THOSE SHAIBAH BLUES

A pictorial memory of service life at

RAF Shaibah – Iraq

1949–1951

BY

COLIN R. MAYES

Published by

MELROSE BOOKS

An Imprint of Melrose Press Limited
St Thomas Place, Ely
Cambridgeshire
CB7 4GG, UK
www.melrosebooks.co.uk

FIRST EDITION

ISBN   978-1-911280-66-8
epub   978-1-911280-67-5
mob   978-1-911280-68-2

Printed and bound in Great Britain by:
CMP (UK) Ltd, G3 The Fulcrum, Vantage Way
Poole, Dorset, BH12 4NU

Prologue

This is a collection of snapshot memories of two years' National Service in the Royal Air Force, mostly in Iraq, some four years after the end of the Second World War, at a time of comparative peace.

The dangerous years of air raids were gone, when my father could be away fire-watching, or on Home Guard duties in Solihull. Whilst my mother shepherded those at home into the Anderson air raid shelter, with my sister being prised (protesting) from her warm bed after a tiring day at work, we lads would be hastily scrambling into our clothes, often getting into the wrong trousers in the dark. Then, together with our toddler brother, we had to spend hours huddled in the candle or Kelly lamp glow, trying to sleep against the drone of aircraft and whistling of bombs, and the thump, thump of anti-aircraft fire that filled the night and early morning. An all-clear siren signalled a weary return to bed, if there was time.

Having survived all this, and my brothers safely home from their service abroad, my mother was not too keen to see another of her family once more about to do service and get an overseas posting. But my obvious enthusiasm for the adventure ahead finally won her over. My promise to write often was easily kept, and I had taken an old Brownie box camera with me. So I tried to make my dispatches a little more interesting by including a snapshot, with details written on the back, of the places, people and the date that it was taken. These snaps were kept by my mother and on my return, were placed in an album.

The ensuing years in returning to Civvy Street and, once more, to earning a living, followed by romance and the pleasures of setting up home with my wife and raising two lads, kept us fully occupied and content. Now, in semi-retirement, I did a little day dreaming on promoting my snapshots to a more modern album. I thought, what if these pictures could come to life and tell their story, for the amusement of my family and friends, and – who knows? – perhaps some of those airmen who also had the chance to go 'round the bend' at Shaibah.

No. 5 Flight "B" Squadron, 1 R.T. Wing, R.A.F. Prague

July 1946

It has given me much pleasure recording the well-remembered happenings along this trail of self-awakening. The place names used are as then, for these names change with time, and if people's names have been misspelt, I apologise.

There was another reason for this diary, for the Gulf War filled me with much sadness for those caught up in it; the Iraqi levies, civilians and especially the children that I had met in my brief eighteen months. From the Kurdish north, to the south of Basra, they were a strong but gentle people, with life humour and love of family that mirrored the best of human nature.

Contents

CHAPTER 1

On Being Called Up

THE MEDICAL

One day in March 1949, a small brown envelope arrived, inviting me to attend Medical Board No. 1 in Birmingham on 11 April.

Along with many other apprehensive youths of 18 years or more, I duly underwent the undignified poking, prodding and short-arm inspection; the obligatory sample that was requested had lads drinking lots of water and running cold water on their wrists, determined not to have to come back on the following day to perform a basic function they had been able to do from day one.

The inspections took place in one very large hall, with screens provided not for any sense of modesty or privacy, but for the separation of each medical examination. The doctors only had trestle tables and wooden school chairs. The draftees, on an invisible conveyor belt, were finally processed, eventually receiving their National Service Act NS 55a grade card, which contained the barest of information. Grade had to be entered by the chairman himself in red ink, as well as date of birth, height, colour of eyes (mine were blue on the card and hazel on demob) and finally, colour of hair. Despite my history of pleurisy and pneumonia, I felt both relieved and pleased to have passed Grade 1.

Some time later, I underwent an aptitude test to determine which service I would be joining. I can recall that one simple choice was to be made out of three types of fruit, to name the odd one out, but was it by colour, shape or the texture? I was convinced that I could find an argument for all three. I shall never know if I got it right.

REPORTING FOR DUTY

My call-up duly arrived and I was to report to RAF Padgate near Warrington in Lancashire. Armed with a travel warrant, a small suitcase and a pocket full of chocolate, to comfort me during the initial shocks to my way of life, I started a rail journey that both excited and filled me with apprehension. It was soon apparent that I was not alone, for others had received the call. So began a period of my life mapped out by the RAF – no longer in my own control, but in the company of fellow beings all in the same boat, or should I say train. We were met by Padgate NCOs, with three-ton trucks, to spirit us away to our holiday camp.

PADGATE

KITTING OUT AND BULL

On arrival at Padgate our names were called, after which we became part of No. 5 Flight, B Squadron, 1 Recruit Training Wing, and were duly marched off to our allocated billet, kitted out with uniforms, bedding and big black boots with pimples all over, which would disappear in the coming days we were assured. After many nights applying black boot polish with the back of a spoon heated on the stove, and with hard pressure, we managed, somehow, to smooth away the pimples to achieve a cherry blossom shine, which almost satisfied our drill instructors, but forever removed a liking for polishing my footwear. Other delightful duties included button and buckle polishing with endless cans of duraglit, using an issued brass button stick. This was done with great care so as to not to get any of the gunge on one's uniform. The cleaning of webbing and belts came into the daily reckoning, and our evenings were filled with billet duties, such as polishing the floors without polish, using rags wrapped about our feet, bumpering the floor. Others would be attempting to clean the windows with newspapers, or blacking the coal in the bucket to make it look smart and clean. Our uniforms had to be pressed, with a sharp crease for our trousers.

In addition to our own kit, we had to take it in turns to do the two Billet Corporals' boots and uniforms. One Corporal, although not a large man, did enjoy a little boxing with the lads after they had finished their valet work, but on our first sparring bout, alas! I caught him a lucky glance on his nose. 'Very good, airman,' he said with his eyes smarting. I did feel a little marked out, however, over the ensuing weeks, not getting the best of duties allocated. The evening work was usually carried out with the accompaniment of music from the wireless. Perry Como singing 'I want some red roses for a blue lady, Mister florist take my order please' was one to stick in my memory. Regulation haircuts came early on, and the barber asked how you would like it cut, but before you could reply, he had all but scalped you.

FATIGUES

Each flight had to do a week of fatigues, which consisted of all manner of menial tasks, performed to reduce the cost of running the camp, and to instil some basic discipline by the very fear of getting a nasty one, such as cleaning the ablution blocks, cleaning the cookhouse's greasy pots and pans, or large cooking cauldrons that required scouring with boiling hot water and hard scrubbing. I did the latter, plus whitewashing the inside of a very large storeroom, which resulted in about five of us being covered with the white stuff, all over our fatigue overalls, mostly from plenty of horseplay. We were given the first nasty on the very next day; mops and buckets in the bogs.

SQUARE BASHING

Square bashing was a painful experience to a pen-pusher like me, and this applied to most of us, but fortunately it was sprinkled with side events that were highly amusing. One lad in our flight was continually at odds with his uniform; his trousers sliding down as he marched, with his belt and bayonet enjoying a life of their own, parading to a different tune. Those of us in close proximity to him became convulsed, but afraid to outwardly snigger for fear of being ordered to scrub the parade ground with a toothbrush during the NAAFI break. Moses (as he was affectionately known) had a sense of humour and goodwill, and enjoyed the banter.

Even the drill instructors feared that they would not turn this lad into a half-decent performer, and I remember very well the day we were first mustered on the roadway outside the billet. The two Drill Instructors were telling us of public concern, in respect of the use of swear words, and derogatory remarks used during training by instructors, and condemned by a prominent lady whose son had just experienced it. They then spent the next ten minutes using every swear word and expletive, in telling us – the assembled useless appendages – what we could expect in the ensuing eight weeks. The mood lightened somewhat as the Drill Instructors' eyes alighted on the hapless Moses, who stood at ease, his legs well apart, desperately trying to stop his trousers, belt and bayonet going walkabout. The Corporals just looked and looked, then went and consulted their register, and then back to eye Moses. It was a well-rehearsed act. There must be a Moses in every batch, but the assembled flight enjoyed some light relief. One of the instructors asked if he was comfortable, and Moses giggled, 'Yes, Corporal', to which the Instructor said, 'You might be, but I'm not,' and spent a few minutes tightening his belt, and trying to put things tidy. 'Now we have sorted out Tom Mix we can come to attention.'

With a change to his authoritative voice, he yelled, 'ATTENTION! Move to the right in threes, right turn,' and so commenced our initiation.

GUARD DUTIES

Later in our training we had to perform guard duties and I recall a long night spent in a pill box, a hundred yards in from the road, with no barrier to raise, another airman sharing the pill box opposite. Periodically, we would take it in turns to march to the road entrance and back again, which at least helped to stave off the incredible desire to nod off, whilst propped to attention in the box. People came and went, and if we were not sure of their right to enter, we would escort them over to the guard room, which was manned by the Duty Sergeant. One individual had some sort of uniform, which could have been a theatrical costume from HMS *Pinafore*, but the Duty Sergeant explained that he belonged to a servicemen's association. However, we did have some delightful hares or rabbits that popped out to see us as dawn broke. One bonus of guard duty was to be sent to the cookhouse to obtain an urn of tea for the entire guard room contingent. This was a pleasant walk in the night, for this was the month of June, and very mild. The cookhouse aromas awakened our taste buds – the night shift was frying bacon and eggs, as Mother would do, not in some communal tray, but in a frying pan, and we were invited to a feast, which we gladly accepted. Guard duties left you very weary.

The time that you are not on guard should be for sleep, but fully dressed in coarse, working blues; it was not always easy to get a proper rest.

TRAINING, JABS AND SORE THROATS

During training, the whole camp was smitten with an epidemic of tonsillitis, which ruled out sick bay confinement, and any form of mollycoddling. We paraded *en masse*, and then queued for throat painting and aspros. On parade, I felt a little feverish and with the warm sun also making me very sleepy, I did the unthinkable. Whilst stood at ease, I let the rifle slip from my grasp; it was the only sound on the parade ground. Instantly, I made to retrieve the situation and grab the rifle, but the Corporal to the front of me gave a hand signal at his side; unmistakably it said leave it. I performed the next few movements giving a display of semaphore, until the Corporal reunited me with my weapon. Moses was not alone.

Inoculations and vaccinations were included, and these were followed by arms drill. We duly marched up and down the parade ground, with our recently jabbed left arm at a right angle, rifle at the slope for a long period, and then around the camp and back to the parade ground, by which time our left arm had set, and the Drill Corporals knew it. 'Flight, wait for it, wait for it, order, order arms!' You could hear the agony as the arms creaked to a straight position. To escape camp for the first time, you had to be passed fit to represent the Royal Air Force and obtain a pass. Our first was a day pass and spent in Manchester, mainly at the Bellevue Zoo, motor cycle racing and the fairground. A splendid day out, strutting our best uniforms, and out of our working blues and fatigue overalls for a day. Fish and chips out of a bag, on the lookout for any officers and NCOs who would not approve, for you cannot bring your right arm longest way up, shortest way down, to salute an officer whilst carrying a bag of steaming chips.

ASSAULT COURSE

Generally, the assault course was the province of the RAF Regiment, at least for some of the field training on weapons, for dismantling and cleaning of the Sten gun and 303 Lea Enfield Rifle. Some were ex-flying crew, like air gunners who after the War stayed in the Service, often with reduced rank. They seemed to treat us with an air of, 'We know you are having a tough time, so enjoy the field work with us.' However, our Drill Corporals were not in the same vein and managed to enjoy themselves immensely at our expense. It was a very hot summer, but we had some heavy showers, and the course was slippery. After scrambling along ropes, under netting, walking on logs, etc., tired and puffed out, I came to the rope over the pool. Here, there was a slippery run up and a Corporal holding the rope steady for each participant to grab, running, and to launch himself on to the far bank. My Corporal, still rubbing his nose, offered me the muddy, slippery rope with a slight wobble. I grabbed hard the rope, about a foot lower than useful, and sailed across, letting go at the furthest point. Only my toes hit the bank and I slid slowly down into the brown, clay-like sludge. Hoots of laughter came from the previous participants, and a lot of instructors, who enjoyed this part of the course. I stayed to see Moses sail across, but not quite reach the far bank as he did not let go, but like a doomed pendulum, swung for an age before dropping in.

The next obstacle was a brick wall. I was still feeling the effects of a sore throat, and with my boots and clothing full of muddy water, I took a chance when the DIs were not looking and legged it between the huts. Back to my own billet and dry clothes, the mud-covered squad marched back without roll call, so I was not missed.

VOLUNTEERS

I think it was August Bank Holiday, and we were to have our first 48-hour pass; a real chance to get home and indulge ourselves. However, not all could go; a small band had to stay on fatigue duties and would be allowed a 48-hour pass the following week, which seemed a long way off, and not the same at all. Volunteers were selected and I realised, not for the first time, that corporals are like elephants; I had nervously answered, 'Yes, Sergeant,' on my first day to my Corporal who had asked a question; he then asked if I was taking the Michael, but on parade one cannot see who is behind, as earlier we had been in the charge of a Sergeant. It pleased him to have a go at me, and the incident with a clipped nose made me odds-on favourite. He circled, bobbed and weaved up and down the ranks, asked for genuine volunteers first and, surprisingly, got three of the six required, but still required three more. I felt his presence to my rear. Awaiting a hand on my shoulder, he still teased and picked two, only one to go, when he presented himself in front of the flight. 'Only one more,' he said, and I looked straight ahead, not daring to give him hint of my fears. Then he was before me. The colour must have left my cheeks by now and like a praying mantis, he struck home. 'I think that you will do,' he said, smiling straight at me.

NAAFI AND LECTURES

Each day at Padgate you were stretched physically. Two memories stay with me. One was the intense concentration that it required to remain awake during lectures by Medical Officers and Padres. Aircraft recognition was easier, because you were all involved and had to concentrate, for questions would come later, but the former could be in the church hall, or some deliciously cool room, where aching limbs would submit to the unexpected relief, and demented eyeballs would roll in a vain effort to stay open. Usually, these lectures were for a combination of flights, i.e. a squadron of airmen, and the Drill Instructors paced up and down to fetch out the snorers, but usually they went undiscovered as they were awakened by the ensuing disturbance and joined in looking about them for the noisy culprit.

The second memory was of morning NAAFI break, that consisted of time enough to sup a mug of tea and eat a wad, but the queues were so great that by the time you were served your scalding hot cuppa and found a seat, the Drill Instructors had ordered you back on parade.

PASSING OUT PARADE

Finally, after miles of marching, arms drill, aircraft and officer recognition, learning how to lay out your kit and bedding for inspection, maintaining your uniform and rifle, we formed up in flights. With some trepidation and lots of pride, combined as a squadron we marched with Moses past the Commanding Officer and some dignitaries, to the stirring sound of the Royal Air Force March and favourite Air Force tunes.

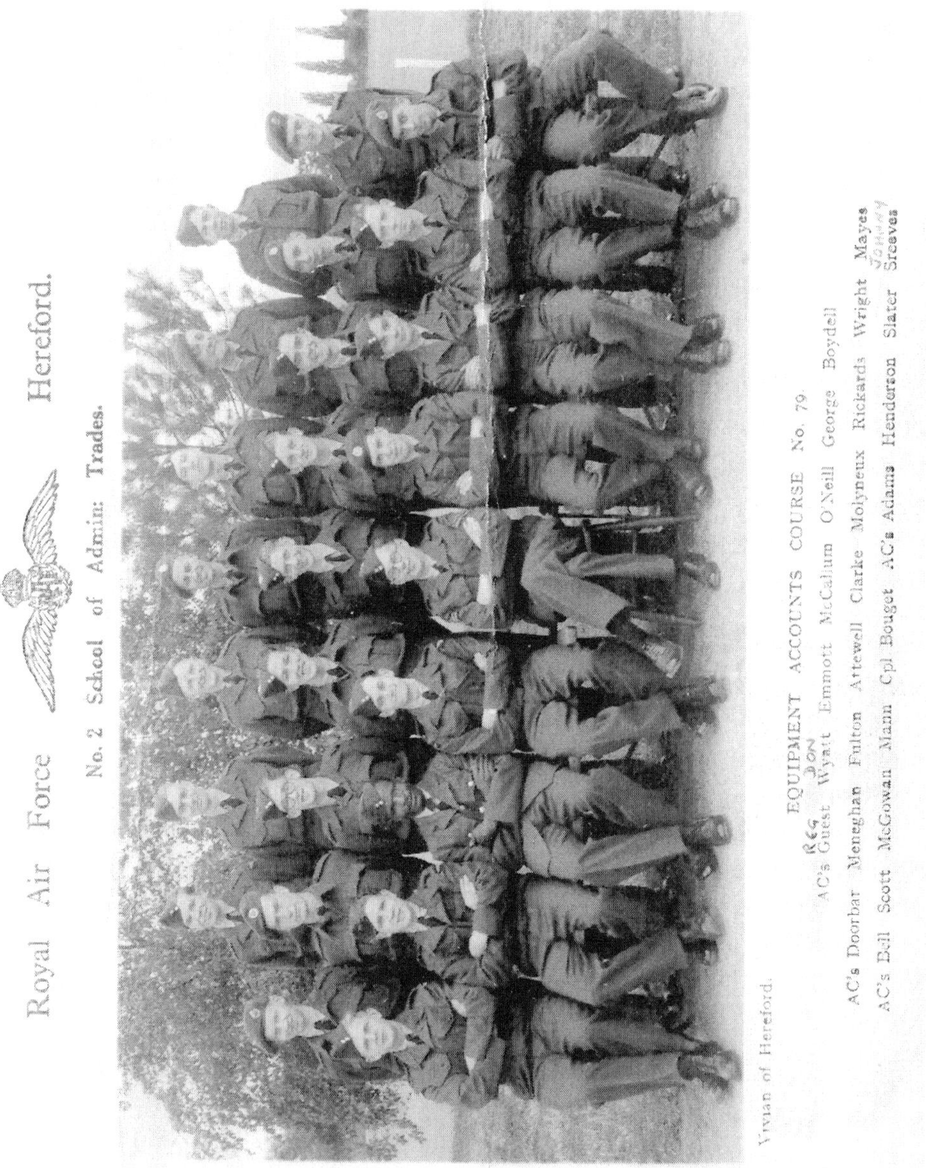

Royal Air Force Hereford.

No. 2 School of Admin: Trades.

Vivian of Hereford.

EQUIPMENT ACCOUNTS COURSE No. 79

AC's Guest Wyatt Emmott McCallum O'Neill George Boydell
 Reg Don

ACs Doorbar Meneghan Fulton Attewell Clarke Molyneux Rickards Wright Mayes

AC's Bell Scott McGowan Mann Cpl Bouget AC's Adams Henderson Slater Sceeves
 Johnny

8

Johnny Sreeves and Don Wyatt

Soldiers three

Reg Guest

Johnny relaxes

CHAPTER 2

Hereford

TRADE TRAINING

After a brief leave, I reported to No. 2 School of Admin Trades RAF Hereford, for training as an equipment clerk. Mainly this consisted of learning the numerous forms and records that float from camp to camp, recording movement of objects by number only, with no record of its monetary value. The forms were in sixes or sevens, I cannot remember exactly. But I do remember that the top was black, the next blue, then red and so on. Each had a function, i.e. one remained on file, one was posted to destination camp, two sent with goods. So on receipt one was matched with a posted voucher, the other copy signed by the Equipment Officer and returned to the sending camp, to square the circle. Other copies were sent to interested area administrative camps, and that was about as exciting as it got.

Hereford Camp was my first initiation into the art of skiving, for between courses we had some mundane duties to perform. The administrative block employed many civilians, including young ladies. So there was a preference to try and get a soft task in the offices – cleaning offices, windows, or as a postman between offices to other parts of the camp. The latter allowed much latitude, as armed with an envelope addressed to, say, the sick bay, one could wander at will for ages, and if challenged, just ask for directions.

POSTINGS AND PREFERENCES

After completing our trade training, and waiting to see if we had passed, preferences for postings were submitted. Four of us who had kept together throughout our time training at Hereford all decided to opt for overseas postings, like Canada, Singapore or Hong Kong. Then we had to undergo further physical tests, to meet overseas requirements. I was the only dodgy applicant, having to confess to a bout of pneumonia in 1948 and several other chest problems during the preceding years. However, I was very relieved to be passed for overseas service, which was a big change to look forward to, as in 1949 travel abroad was not within the pocket of working folk, and Cornwall was about as far as I had ventured to date.

We had our overseas jabs for typhoid, tetanus and so on, which was an experience in itself, having to walk the gauntlet of medical officers and orderlies, armed on both sides with an injection. Mine took two goes on my left arm, saying, 'You've got a very thick skin.' I thought, 'You've got a very blunt needle!' Then they splodged some purple-looking dye under our armpits and told us to have a quiet night in, as we might feel slightly feverish for a bit. I did and went to bed early. On 12 October I had entered in my 'Form 64' Airman's Service and Pay Book, 'Trade – Clerk Equipment Accounts,' and a day later as Aircraftman Second Class I was at last a little somebody.

CHAPTER 3

Hednesford

EMBARKATION

After embarkation leave, I arrived at Rugeley after a short journey by train from New Street station, then was taken by truck to 5 PDC Hednesford for my final preparation for overseas service. After the initial scramble for a bunk, collecting three straw biscuits, blankets and sheets, I bedded down for the night, reflecting on the adventure ahead and the loved ones' farewells. One among our four on the course had a steady girl and needed extra cheering up.

The following days were taken up in obtaining overseas kit, which at least gave some clue as to whether a warm or cold clime was in the offing and that was all. We all four had khaki drill – not Canada, I thought – and on 10 November further jabs, including yellow fever, meant farewell to Canada. We had an addition to our kit in the form of yet another kit-bag, this time with two pale blue rings around it, on to which we then had to stencil our service number, name and other details, as this was the 'not wanted on voyage' bag. We also drew a metal, cloth-covered, hip-slung water bottle of the Gunga Din type, and, thus prepared, we were looking for the next oasis.

HARWICH TO THE HOOK OF HOLLAND

After travelling to Harwich, arriving at dusk we duly boarded our ship, and after eats, fell into sleep with ease in our cramped bunk beds. Close to the noise and vibrations of the engines, weary from a day man-handling kit bags and a small pack on our backs, we fell into oblivion. On awakening, we had already started to enter the approach to the Hook of Holland and before long, I set foot for the first time on foreign soil. I was not disappointed to see workmen outside the camp wearing clogs just to confirm.

However, the transit camp was equipped with communal toilets, which were centre-room in rows, back to back and shoulder high, so no smell or sound could be discreetly dealt with. Looking straight ahead we sat like broody hens, not caring to look at one's neighbour. In such circumstances we performed as best we could. Washed and refreshed, we made our way to the more pleasant aromas of food. Here we were served by local Dutch girls, some quite young. This was our first breakfast not served by some pimply airman, busily scratching his bum and serving boiled eggs of a slightly green hue. One attractive young lady serving our table was asked by a still hungry airman, 'Can I have some more, love?' to which she replied, 'The bacon on your plate was more than we saw in a month during the War!' That remark made us all feel a little guilty.

MEDLOC – HOLLAND TO TRIESTE

This was the name given to the route overland, which took us by train south through Holland, Germany, Austria to Trieste, travelling through some very green and beautiful plains and forests around Munich. Then, in contrast, through Bavarian snow-capped mountains we climbed, where the train halted high up for a brief stay, just long enough to hop out for a snowball fight. On our gradual descent, the train slowed down, through one long stretch of tunnel and looking out of the window, we observed cavern-like openings in which men were engaged on rail maintenance. In the lantern glow they looked like the seven dwarfs at work in their diamond mine.

We stayed for food at Villach, before continuing the last part of the journey by rail to Trieste. Here, we were required to march some distance, from the train to the awaiting troopship. Encumbered with the extra kit-bag, it was exhausting. We still had time, however, to take in the impressive views of Trieste; the calm, blue water so peaceful only a few feet below the promenade. The good ship SS *Westralia* stood ready, but access to the ship now towering above us consisted of a series of steep walkways, or gangplanks, reaching to the sky. With two kit-bags, it meant shouldering one and dragging the other, freeing a hand to grip the rail; it was hot, slow and tortuous.

SS *WESTRALIA* – TRIESTE TO PORT SAID

This ship was our home from 20–23 November. In the main, it was one of the most pleasurable periods to date, as it required long stints of card-playing on deck, gambling with matches representing a small stake, and generally soaking up the sun. Occasional bouts of duty were expected, such as replenishing the galley with its daily requirement of sides of beef, lamb, pork, vegetables or fruit, fetched from the bowels of the ship, up endless stairways. The sea was so calm we sat as near to the bow of the ship as possible, to try and get some feeling of movement. Some who came via the Bay of Biscay retched all the way. Nevertheless, there were cases of sea sickness early on in the journey and, as it could be difficult to find a vacant loo in an emergency, this required lots of nervous searching of the decks for a kindly vacant one. I spent almost all of the time that was possible on deck, including the evenings until quite late, before soaking in the smells of close bodies, in bunks below decks, where I felt somewhat claustrophobic. I can remember seeing rows of Coca-Cola bottles riding well astern, left bobbing in the blue waters of the Mediterranean, some with an invented message sealed inside.

SS Westralia

EGYPT – PORT SAID

Before sighting Port Said and the entrance to the Suez Canal, I was amazed to see, on land, what appeared to be row after endless row of military hardware, tanks and trucks, as far as the eye could see. The debris of war, each cocooned in dusty sand, each with a tale to tell of heroism and hardship. Port Said was like a watery anthill, for every way one turned there were ships and boats of all shapes and sizes, covered with people of all nationalities and colour. We stood by our belongings, waiting to disembark, being harassed by men in bumboats, to buy watches, wallets and all manner of clothing. One abnormally well-endowed young man gave the buyers a Full Monty between sending up samples by a rope, thrown up to the high decks and, hopefully, receiving payment by the same method. He was proud of what he had, and coins were dropped for his efforts to entertain us. We disembarked via some kind of pontoon and finally put foot on Egyptian soil, then made our way to a very large warehouse building, where we were sorted into destinations. Our four from the equipment accounts course were spread all over the Middle East. We made our hasty goodbyes and 'keep in touch' promises, which we kept to some extent afterwards. Don got the plum posting to Cyprus, Johnny stayed in Egypt, Reg went to Aden and I was posted to Iraq.

EGYPT – EL HAMRA AND FAYID

We then boarded a troop train, still jostled by Arab salesmen so vigorously, in fact, that the military police and NCOs in charge were literally trying to boot them off as they clung by every window. I was at the rear of the train and with the end connecting door open saw, with the train gathering pace, the last and most tenacious of the salesmen fall away. RAF El Hamra was, for me, a short staging post on my awaited flight to Iraq, and after collecting bedding plus a lamp, I was allocated a tent and left to discover, with my new companions, the amenities of the camp. Whilst wandering all over the sprawling camp, we came across a Warrant Officer putting some senior officers through a refreshment training course, in true drill instructor fashion, although each order was preceded with the courtesy of, 'Gentlemen will you please move to the right in threes, right turn,' and 'Perhaps you could have done that a little sharper, Mister Brown, sir!'

After NAAFI beers it became easy to sleep in our tent under the stars, for it had been a long and eventful day. Next morning, after breakfast, I reported to transit reception, to be told to return bedding to store and be ready for transport to Fayid. Arriving at Fayid about lunchtime, I was ushered into a mess hall and served by a splendid figure with turban, white tunic and cummerbund. I was on my own, and felt that I had strayed into a film of the North West Frontier. I much enjoyed the meal and being waited upon; however, after a while, I was ordered to report to reception as the flight was cancelled and would be returning to El Hamra. There, I had to once more get some bedding, an oil lamp, and spend another night in the transit camp.

SHIPS THAT PASS

El Hamra was also the camp where, some years earlier, my brother Victor had spent most of his service as corporal in the equipment section. My eldest brother, George, was to come through the Suez Canal on his way home from service as a wireless operator in India and, as it was then called, Ceylon. It happened that Victor had the opportunity of travelling down to Port Tuafiq at the southern end of the canal, escorting some sick personnel who were being shipped home on the *Cameronian*. He actually went out to the ship in an attempt to see his brother, George, on board, as it lay at anchor in the Gulf of Suez, but some army officer said quite sharply, 'We take over from here!' probably fearing someone might be tempted to stay aboard for Blighty. The *Cameronian* had torpedo damage, and had to journey from Colombo and Bombay at a slow list. The full journey took about four weeks, and it arrived to a great reception at Glasgow where she had been built. Victor was finally reunited with George after a gap of nearly five years, at the end of his service in 1948. Just over one year later, I was at the same camp and on the Suez Canal, where their ship had passed in 1947. The following day, I dined once more at the 'North West Frontier' mess and awaited my transport to Habbaniya in Iraq.

CHAPTER 4

Egypt – Jordan – by Hastings to Habbaniya

On 25 November 1949, after a splendid meal at the Fayid mess, I was ordered to report to reception and then directed to the airstrip; there a Hastings aircraft awaited me. Upon climbing aboard, I discovered that I was to be the only passenger, apart from an ATC cadet who had won some award and was having a tour of Air Force life. We settled down ready for take-off, quite excited at my first flight. The aircraft trundled across to the runway, which seemed to take forever, and for a while, I lost myself in some book that I had become engrossed in. The throbbing engines began to rev up, then to tick over, awaiting clearance for take-off. Again more revs as the whole aircraft seemed to be vibrating and alive. Then more settled, I took a look through the window and, to my astonishment, we were already aloft. The airfield support vehicles and waiting aircraft looked like Dinky models. I was not aware that we had left the ground, for these mighty beasts had a more even take-off than the modern jets.

Once in the air, my companion and I set about finding the best vantage points to observe and snap the views. The aircrew took it in turns to come back to explain the route and point out certain landmarks to us. Firstly, we had to fly south-east over the Sinai Peninsula, avoiding the Israeli Negev desert and then over the Gulf of Aqaba, and port of the same name. Then, north-east over Jordan, we saw both the hilly terrain and open desert below us. Avoiding Saudi Arabia, we flew due east to Iraq. The area flown over had seen the Arab Revolt in 1917, during which Aqaba was captured from the Turks. Later in April 1941, a relief column had, with all manner of troops and transport, set out from Jordan to Iraq to relieve the Air Force base at Habbaniya (our destination) under siege from Iraqi troops. These were led by Raschid Ali, an ex-premier with an allegiance to the Germans. Some years later, I met a Mr Barnett, one of the men who took part in this trek. He recalled that it was a very exciting journey and that having come out unscathed, it remained the most vivid memory of his life and was glad to have taken part. We arrived at RAF Habbaniya with a less exhausting journey in our Hastings, which I always recall had wings that moved perceptively up and down during the flight. This, the crew assured me, was normal movement.

HABBANIYA

TRANSIT CAMP

Upon arrival, I was ensconced in a large tent with two other airmen awaiting their flight out the next morning. The weather took a turn for the worse, and it rained very heavily that night. After a drink or two in the NAAFI, I fell fast asleep and awoke the next morning to find that I was encircled by water a few inches deep. My kit had been thoughtfully placed on a spare bunk by the other two who had already departed to catch their early flight, so I made my way barefoot to the ablution block for an early morning shave. Breakfast in the camp was very good, I being the only one in transit. I had the pick of the food on the tables, which always consisted of some fresh fruit – usually limes and grapes, etc. – then, after a double egg and bacon, I was ready to explore the camp. I did have to let reception know where I was going, and to check in from time to time in case my next move came through.

Hastings wing over Jordan

Hastings engines over Jordan

Jordan

LOST DIGNITY

However, my bowels helped to shape events, and ensured a longer stay in transit than was normal, for after a long breakfast I paid a visit to the toilet in a separate block to the rear of the transit reception. Hanging my jacket on a coat hook on the partition directly behind me, I had a refreshing wash. Then a call of nature was indicated, so I went to the lavatory behind the partition wall. No sooner had I sat down, with my trousers around my ankles, than the outer fly door banged to with a resounding thud and I knew instantly that I had foolishly left my jacket unattended. Shuffling straight out, I placed my hand on my empty jacket pocket, then descended into the pit of despair. All my worldly goods had gone. My wallet, a few Dinars and some notes of 250 and 500 fils, worth perhaps a fiver, or in other words, two weeks' spending money. More seriously though, my Form 64 Royal Air Force airman's service and pay book, detailing rank, medical details, inoculations, etc., had also gone. I composed myself as best I could, as the instructions to airmen on page one of the pay book are clearly stated:

21

1. You will be held personally responsible for the safe custody of this book.
2. You will always carry the book on your person at home and abroad.

Did this include going to the toilet?

Some short time later, I finally had the attention of the Transit Sergeant and blurted out my pathetic tale. After a pregnant pause he said, 'You are very lucky, airman. One of our levy guards spotted an Arab lad hiding something in one of the unused tents. He took him and your wallet to the levy's SHQ. They notified me even before you reported it stolen.'

Very relieved and sheepish, I thanked the Sergeant and, later, the Iraqi levy for their good work.

However, I did not immediately realise the impact that this small incident would have on my situation. Firstly, I was transported to the levy's SHQ to retrieve my goods. Here, a levy officer was taking a statement from the Guard, which was taken down in Arabic script, right to left (or back to front), and was fascinating to watch when giving my own story to see it unfold in Arabic. I wished that I could keep it, for it was like a work of art. On asking how long before my transportation to my allotted posting, I was staggered to learn that I would be required to wait in transit until the case was heard before the Juvenile Magistrates in Ramadi, a town the other end of Lake Habbaniya. I was now beginning to realise what a mess it all was.

SMOKING

My enforced stay under canvas for four weeks, mainly on my own, started me smoking, which I had avoided up until now, apart from youthful experiments with dog-ends in clay pipes, or a pack of five shared Willie Woodbines. The reason for my starting came about because, from time to time, Customs and Excise would release some of their confiscated contraband for re-sale at a small charge, with the proceeds going to the RAF Benevolent Fund and sometimes given out free at Christmas. As we were soon coming up to Christmas, I came in for a free issue of one pack of 50 Players and one 50 Senior Service can of cigarettes. You took a chance on their quality, depending on the length of time they had been stored, or if the can was punctured or not. You could open the can and find green musty ones, but mine were good, unfortunately, so I began a career as a smoker that lasted until some 30 years ago.

GUARD DUTIES

The regular task I became an expert at was that of guard duty, for the Transit Sergeant thought it best to keep me usefully employed doing something other than eating, sleeping and smoking. I therefore did several guard duties each week, and got to know the military police and levies quite well. The levies were under their own officers and orders; they patrolled the perimeter rather than guarding one spot. The camp perimeter was huge, and consisted of a high wire and mesh fencing, with the occasional gateway to the outer world. On one of these gateways stood a turret, large enough for about four bods, which I shared for the night with a fellow volunteer, each with a .303 Rifle and I think ten rounds of ammunition. The turret was of brick or stone and had its slits in the outer wall for peering out of, as well as for firing through, with the obligatory stove to keep us cosy and brew a cuppa. We took it in turns to step outside and stretch our legs, keeping a wary eye out for signs of the Duty Officer in his 15cwt truck, trying to surprise us, or the military police, who on occasion would come up on horseback, usually in pairs, to unlock the gate and disappear for an hour or so, reputedly to search the outer areas and shoot wild dogs we called piards. We did in fact hear shooting, but they were probably having a bit of practice. All night long, we heard the sounds of the dogs, crickets and frogs.

Only eight years earlier, Raschid Ali had bombarded this camp in an attempt to oust the British, who had initially only training aircraft that had to be adapted to carry bombs. They were then reinforced by a mixture of Audaxes, Gladiators, Oxfords and Gordons, and held out until the relief column called Habforce had crossed the desert via Amman to reach Habbaniya in May 1941. This campaign ensured a vital and strategic presence in the Middle East and its vital oil fields for Britain but, for some reason, never had its days of heroism and glory truly recorded for public recognition, perhaps because many of the heroes were only instructors or trainees and not Colonel Blimps. This would surely have made an exciting film, and could have been made when such aircraft were still available. Of course, I was not aware of this history of Habbaniya at the very moment I was guarding it with my ten rounds. Some ten years after my visit, the Royal Air Force was to leave Habbaniya, along with all their other bases in Iraq.

CAMEL RACES AND GARDEN LAWNS

I was able to explore, in my free time, the extent of this prestigious RAF camp, which had many miles of roads. The camp had its own taxi service, a civilian village with many shops, riding stables, a polo pitch, many tennis courts, a large swimming pool and even its own racecourse, which I was able to see in action as a race meeting took place whilst I was still there. I also saw, for the first and only time, serious camel racing, where the jockeys seemed to be about ten years old and glued to the bums of these magnificent creatures who appeared to sail along effortlessly around the track at a tremendous lick.

One of my favourite walks took me past the married quarters, which had irrigation ditches surrounding magnificent lawns edged by eucalyptus trees, shrubbery and very green gardens amidst the desert. On this walk, there were large areas of open land with Arab youngsters tending livestock and, in a very shaded road, St Mary's Catholic Church stood in what could have been a rural British scene. Many years later, I spoke to a lady who had spent some of her childhood with her parents in the married quarters and remembered the ditches with horror as a neighbour's child had drowned in one. It was a remarkable coincidence that, on comparing the time of my stay at Habbaniya, this lady was also there as a young girl at the very same time.

RAMADI

MAGISTRATES AND GUILT

Eventually, I was on my way to Ramadi in a 15cwt truck, with a sergeant of the military police, the levy, and for the first time I saw the young Arab boy that had taken my wallet. I was gutted and could not speak for quite a while. The Sergeant explained to me that the problem was one of religion and, as the lad was a Jew would accordingly, in his opinion, be more sorely dealt with. The lad was in the care of his grandfather who had gone to Baghdad on business and had not had any parental control for some time, and was now very contrite.

We awaited our time outside the court, with the world and his wife debating, haranguing and swearing in Arabic around the courtyard, for there were lawyers with the accused and plaintiffs, all sorting themselves out for the various cases of wife beating, wife desertion and property squabbles, etc. Finally, we were all ushered in and the formalities began, after a long and lengthy reading of our statements in both languages, which we had to confirm. The Sergeant put in his heart-warming plea for the youngster, who finally had a fine imposed, although I never knew how much. On our return trip, I was much relieved and relaxed until passing a gang of chained prisoners walking along the road after their day's toil, including quite young men. The Sergeant said, 'I'm glad that they did not hold him, for he is old enough to be with them.' The young lad looked more and more angelic, as I stole a glance at him, and I felt more like the villain. Then, at last, I had my posting travel warrant for Shaibah.

BAGHDAD

BY TRAIN TO SHAIBAH

On 22 December 1949, I joined a party of airmen who were also bound for Shaibah and Basra. We piled into a three-ton truck for a dusty drive of about 45 miles to Baghdad, via Falluja. I recall seeing a solitary camel and its rider covered up against the biting dust storm, heading in the same direction, leaving the vision to the care of his trusty steed, for he seemed to be asleep. We gradually left him behind. Unfortunately, at this time, we were not able to see anything of the fabled city of Baghdad as we made straight for the station. There, we were allocated our carriage for the journey, which contained overhead bunks, thereby sleeping four of us. Some time after leaving the station, an attendant came to the carriage with fresh, iced water, who told us of the evening meal time and the location of the dining car.

We had, by now, become accustomed to carrying with us the standard knife, fork, spoon and enamel mug, when meal times beckoned, but not now. After struggling past several carriages crammed with families of Arabs, all engaged in their own meal time preparations, chapattis and all manner of fruits, we made our way to the dining car.

The dining car had, to us, the class of old-time luxury one expected to see on the Orient Express. To sit at a table with a table cloth, glasses, a pitcher of water and nice cutlery, the meal that followed was great and memorable. We sat for a long time, watching the other travellers, some in traditional robes and head gear; some in city suits. All colour and creeds chattered away like mad, including us, for there is an international love of travel by train that seems to exercise the senses; to us novices it was the honey pot. The evening descended with varying shades across the open landscape, until the desert light was suddenly put out and replaced by an inky blue sky full of bright stars.

We retired to our carriage and took a beer, or two, before settling down with our many kit-bags on the floor. We stretched out on our two-up, two-down sleeper, securing the window shutters to keep out the unrelenting dust. We all awoke early and opened up the shutters to reveal a vista of desert, the occasional oasis and many date palms. Most station halts resembled the Wild West, with one long hut and a water tower. They all seemed to have a crowd of lads, willing to race the train as it left the station, until it got up steam and left them only in the memory. After our ablutions, we again visited the dining car for breakfast. Our journey south concluded just short of Basra, if memory serves me correctly, at Shu'aiba Junction. A very different phase of my service life was about to commence.

Habbaniya – children and their mules

St Mary's Catholic Church, Habbaniya

RAF Military Police

Arab's tote

Parade ring

British personnel tote

Camels at the post

CHAPTER 5

Shaibah

Arriving at Shu-aiba Junction on Friday 23 December 1949, we stepped out of the train into an awaiting truck and were soon introduced to the way of life at this small outpost. It was very different to the lush and well-appointed Habbaniya I had just left. The SHQ staff took my details and allotted me to a billet, in which other 'store bashers' resided, and before long, I was one of the family. As a newcomer, I was subjected to all the usual advice and horror stories of life at Shaibah, but at least I had a more permanent home, after a month sleeping in tents.

I had arrived at a good time to see the camp in a festive mood, for this was one day before Christmas Eve. I was escorted to the NAAFI in the late afternoon and was somewhat surprised to see an airman on a plank between two step ladders, completely naked, putting up Christmas decorations, bellowing forth to the tune of a well-known Irish ballad:

> Just a little bit of heaven fell, from out of the sky one day,
> It settled in the ocean, oh so very far away,
> And when the Airforce saw it, sure, it looked so bleak and
> bare,
> They said that's what we're looking for; we'll build our
> airfield there.
> So they sprinkled it with airmen, armoured cars, and SHQ.

There are numerous versions of this song and also of Shaibah's own verse:

> We've got those Shaibah blues, Shai-bah blues,
> We're fed up, we're f...d up, we're cheesed.

I soon became aware that this was a male-only camp with no married quarters, and no females residing within the camp (even our dogs and horses were male), so the freedom was there for us to behave badly, if we so wished. Here, I learned to swear, as no one took much notice of you without the odd expletive to enforce your argument. This bad language helped to assuage the many frustrations that servicemen feel away from home comforts; I needed some time to readjust when back in Civvy Street, not to let the odd word slip out during my duties as a respectable audit clerk.

CHRISTMAS 1949

Christmas upon us, and memories of home affected some individuals very badly. They were sad and morose, and needed a little chivvying to get into the party spirit. Requests from home on our camp's tannoy system did not always help. However, doing the rounds of visiting the various billets, sampling a drink at each one, before enjoying our Christmas dinner (served by the officers), ensured the right mood was reached. Arriving at this time helped me familiarise myself with the camp layout and the various sections, not that the occupied area was that big for it supported less than a hundred Air Force person-nel. I found the large hangars and spacious airstrip very impressive, being the first operational airfield, apart from Fayid, that I had seen at close quarters. There were the RAF Iraqi levies, with their own offic-ers under British command, there to defend the camp, as no British military forces, other than the RAF, were allowed in Iraq. There was an exception; a small contingent of Army engineers (about four or five), their prime purpose being to maintain the communication lines. Shaibah had a contingent of Baluchi Guards, who had their own quar-ters alongside the main camp; their duties consisted of guarding the extensive outer perimeter wire. The camp had been used during the War as a staging post to ferry aircraft parts and supplies to Russia, and had also accommodated Prisoners of War at some time. A Shaibah posting was of a limited period only, to reduce the chances of airmen going 'round the bend'.

Arriving on the Friday, and Christmas Day being Sunday, I did not have to take up my duties until the Tuesday when I reported to the Equipment Officer, Flight Lieutenant Wareham, and was quickly put at ease. I had a desk with the pigeon holes already bulging with unmatched documents awaiting my deliberations. 'You've taken your time getting here,' I was told. 'The airman you're replacing has been gone several weeks, so there's some catching up to do. Here's a list of old shipments I know we should have received and cleared; see if you can make some progress with them.'

STORE BASHING AND MATES

My early days, which turned into weeks, and then months, were spent looking for these elusive shipments, but were a blessing in disguise, as I spent much of my time outside the equipment section. Firstly, I checked at the main store, checking all items for hidden blue and red forms, and soon found enough to prove I was really looking and not just skiving off. The real bonus was that some supplies came via Basra, which enabled me to get some visits when supplies were sent for, to roam around this camp in search of any possible missing goods. This gave me some pleasurable walks along the riverside, where the camp had a jetty to fish from. I was shown, whilst there, a small shark in an ice box, caught that morning. I do not know what they intended to do with it. I was fortunate in having some very good mates, mainly from the equipment section – Charles Tomes, Ginger Pepper, Ali Dyer, Roy Ison, Jim Forte, Sid Sawyer, Johnny McGuigan, Les Jarman, Tony Hibbet, Don Kavanagh, Corporal Brian Glover and Sergeant Nott, also of the equipment section, were included in many a good party.

The section had an Iraqi Kurd named Abbas, who (though not tall) was built like the proverbial brick toilet. He displayed his strength by lying on the floor and lifting, one-handed, a wooden chair by its leg, using the power of his wrist up in the air. On one occasion, whilst trying to move some rail trucks by pushing them alone and unaided, he found that he was unable to do so and was getting quite annoyed, until the offending brake, put on in jest, was found and duly released. He had travelled south when quite young; I asked if he would like to return to Kurdistan and the mountains of the north, to which he replied, 'Of course, if the work is there, and if I have enough money for the fare.' He was not able to save money and when asked why not, he squirmed visibly and explained that on pay day he spent most of his money on a weekend binge of food and drink. Then, laughing sheepishly, he said 'and much lovely vimmins'.

WAR SURPLUS PARTY

We had a mass of equipment in a large area next to the kerosene compound, consisting of wartime remnants, many trucks, and all manner of transport and military hardware that the Air Force were slowly disposing of, mainly for scrap, for it was probably not on any inventory. The Arab traders would come and make their bids for the items which they would tow away in a truck filled with radio and other equipment. Weeks later, that scrapped truck would return to tow more loads away. As well as paying the RAF for the scrap, they used to bring goodies in the shape of grapes, sugar and water melons, and a few bottles of spirits; these were split between the officers, sergeants and the equipment section. After an accumulation of these spirits, our Sergeant arranged a party for the equipment section. The party was held on one weekend morning, and after trying a cocktail of brandy, whisky and crème de menthe, my stomach began to give me warnings, but nevertheless, I, with others, made our way to the canteen for dinner and our lot stood out as a swaying mass of tipsy rowdies. I could never refuse soup if on the menu, so I sat down next to Charlie, who had a smile on his face, but was in a land far away. He said, 'Hello, me mate,' and promptly nodded off. We pulled him off his soup and I took one look at my bowl of brown soup which had little shiny grease rings dancing merrily away, and felt an uncontrollable urge to refund all my morning's samples, which I did, just about making the sand outside the mess hall. After a while, I returned to see all were in a pretty sorry state. Charlie and I staggered back to our billet supporting each other. His knees would give way from time to time as he was a bit more under the influence, having the spirits still within him, but we reached our bunks. After sobering up a little, we found that one of our lads had not returned, so we sent a search party out and found him still fast asleep at the mess table. It was decided to borrow a wheelbarrow to bring him back in a dignified manner with his own guard in attendance. Still a little the worse for drink, we kept falling into some irrigation ditches along the way. I do not remember being so affected by drink ever again; surely it was a sobering experience.

SHOPS AND WALKS

There may not have been much in the way of amenities on the camp (the civilian shops I can barely recall to mind), but it did have a camp barber, and a tailor's shop where you could have made-to-measure Egyptian-cotton shirts, so very useful. He had several pith helmets that were once standard issue at this camp; I always regretted not buying one as a memento from Mesopotamia. One of the shops where we had our films developed sold photographs of public executions and punishments, which were graphic and horrible.

As for entertainment, long walks provided one cheap way of passing the time, but there were not a lot of beauty spots to visit, except for one location, which was not beautiful but worthy of a good trek, to visit the Shu'aiba Forts. This we did on New Year's Day, which was a Sunday. These forts were a few miles from camp, and a small party of enthusiasts set forth across the hard stony desert, visiting the fort railway station on the way. Whilst at one of the two forts, and up one of the few remaining turret stairways, I was reminded of one of my favourite films – 'Beau Geste'. And so this was Fort Zinderneuf to me; I could hear the sounds of the last post being played by a tearful bugler. Looking down, I saw a pack of wild dogs on the far side of the forts. My heroic moment dissolved and I was glad to get back to the comparative safety of numbers at an Arab smallholding. Here, we were amazed at the simple efficiency of an irrigation scheme that consisted of three pulleys above a well, driven by mules on a slope downwards away from the well, whilst the goatskin bags were hauled up, which deposited the water into an awaiting trough. Sluice-gates then directed the water to the appropriate channel and the mules then returned back up the slope, endlessly repeating the operation.

Another walk, and somewhat further, was to visit Zubair, the only town in walking distance from the camp. The shortcut to avoid a longer trek by road was about three miles, I think, and required a little effort as we crossed very rough ground. On one visit, the water hollows were all severely dried up and we fell about acting out the *Four Feathers* scenes, staggering from each hollow, cracked in mosaic-like patterns, crying out for water. The town of Zubair had shops, mosques, minarets, hawk sellers and a marketplace selling everything. Not that we had much money to spend, but there was a quite respectable barber's shop in which you would be served scalding hot tea in a small, thin glass that burned your sun-hot hands. Very refreshing once cooled a little. If two of you had haircuts, about six could enjoy a free cuppa whilst waiting.

Shu'aiba Junction

Geordie and Charlie

Aerial view of RAF Shaibah

SHQ – MT and Equipment sections

Shu'aiba Fort No. 1

Shu'aiba Fort No. 2

Jim at the top of the Shu'aiba well

Water for the sluices

Zubair Minaret

Zubair police

Ginger in alley to mosque

Hawk seller

Tour of ruins

Street musician

Ali Dyer, Cpl Wright, Charlie, Geordie, Eddie Reg, Ginger, Ossie, Cpl Brian Glover, Johnny and Frankie

Zubair's ancient ruins

Flight Sergeant Nott – Self, Ali Dyer, Ossie and Jim

Syd, Chas, Eddie, Pete, Bill, Les and Reg

A walk through Zubair

Ali Dyer, Cpl Wright, Charlie, Geordie, Eddie,
Reg, Ginger, Ossie, Cpl Brian Glover, Johnny and Frankie

Billet 23b

Self, Charlie, Hamet, Mahli and Juma

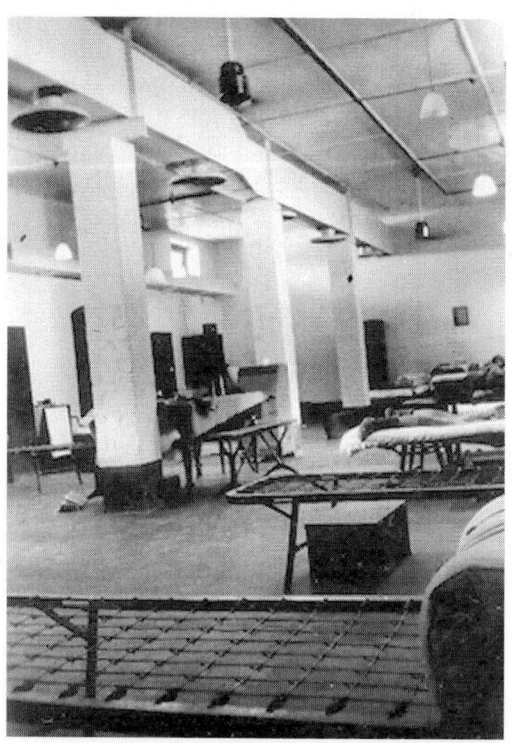

Our Shaibah home

May 1950 – Floods after hurricane

Airfield tower and billet damage

MT Billet South

MT Billet North

Pool shop damage

Officers' 'Mess'

CHAPTER 6

Shaibah

RAF REGIMENT

During my stay at Shaibah, we had a visit by the RAF Regiment, in various armoured cars and trucks, on their way to Kuwait to do a bit of flag waving at some important event. Their stay, though short, disrupted life for a while as they were intent on impressing us with their toughness – for had they not just driven from Habbaniya, some 300 miles in the desert heat, and slept under the stars? However, they pushed their way everywhere and grabbed several rounds of bread at a time, unlike us more refined admin, fitters and store wallahs. At last they departed, but not before some fights had occurred, and we were glad they did not re-visit us on their way back.

BILLET BOYS

On April Fool's Day, I finally became an aircraftsman 1st class, and earned a few more fils to help pay for the daily expenses, one of which consisted of a payment to our billet boy, Mahli, who was assisted by his young cousin, Hamet. They were on attendance from early morning, polishing shoes and providing hot water from the mess for shaving and so on, and if you left yesterday's sweaty clothes at the foot of the bed, by midday they were then folded and ironed. This was a most civilised arrangement, and all paid for on pay day, costing us little individually, but a billet-full provided a real wage. When I say it cost us little, we were paid little, so proportionately I suppose that it was about all we could afford. These two became as part of the billet family. Mahli was to wed during our stay. He always giggled with embarrassment when quizzed about his coming marriage, while little Hamet always had so large a smile even at an early hour, quietly polishing one's boots or shoes.

GUARD DUTIES

There were, of course, extra duties to perform after the daily equipment section work, which started about 8.30am and finished in the very hottest part of the year at about midday. The hours varied according to the time of year. These extra chores consisted of duty clerk and main gate guard, the latter I had been well trained to do at Habbaniya. It consisted of sharing the late afternoon to morning with another airman on the main gate, to scrutinise all folk in and out of the camp. We did have two RAF levies manning the pole barrier and vetting the civilians who worked on the camp as they left at night and reappeared next morning. On taking turns throughout the night to get a little shut-eye on a bunk in a side room, one had to spend some time killing off some of the more obnoxious bugs and large moths that infested the room, attracted by the floodlights that illuminated the gateway. Occasionally, the quiet of the night would be broken when a festival or wedding was taking place in the civil cantonment, a camp just opposite to the guard room, and from where music and singing could be heard.

Sometimes, on very warm nights, children would come to talk and play beneath the lights. Then, the mornings grew colder as the silent, low dawn mist spread like a Hammer Horror and disembodied early morning workers approaching the camp. Their heads were seen a long time before their bodies, and the small children with them became visible, and then their chatter as they passed woke up the day.

DUTY CLERK AND THE DIPLOMATIC BAG

The other duty, carried out on a roster, consisted of drawing a Sten gun from the armoury and taking over the SHQ and Pay office, to stop anyone getting at the dosh, but also to be there to assist the Duty Officer if needs be in an emergency. One could have company during the evening in moderation; we usually took it in turns to visit those on duty to see if they needed anything from the NAAFI. The duty also required that the Daily Routine Orders be typed on a Gestetner skin, with one copy printed off for proof reading next morning by the admin wallahs. I, being a slow one-finger typist, took most of the night to complete it, the red corrector patches on the skin looking as if I had shed blood on its creation.

Duty clerk could be on the weekend as well as night time, and on two separate occasions the duty Dakota arrived with some diplomatic mail, once for the British Consulate in Basra. This required me to notify the Duty Officer, who obtained another Duty Clerk to replace me, then notified the Duty Driver to draw two rifles and to convey me and the diplomatic bag to Basra. This was done without mishap and earned a glass of lemonade at the Consulate, an empty bag to take back with a duly signed receipt, and off we set back to Shaibah. However, the driver had forged some sort of liaison with a lady in Asher, which is a part of Basra, and left me to sit it out in the truck with the two rifles while he popped in for a visit. I sat there for the best part of an hour, gripping my rifle in one hand and holding a clip of bullets in the other. Fortunately, the doors were locked, but I dared not open a window as numerous young men were all over the truck, and even in the open-ended rear. Eventually, very pleased with himself, he returned, quite oblivious of my worries.

On another occasion, I had to take the diplomatic bag for one of the navy ships; it could have been the *Mauritius*, as they did entertain us with a Royal Marine Band display while I was there, as well as challenging us to hockey and other such sports, but the ship I actually boarded was, I think, a small escort ship. I can remember the brilliant-white uniforms of all the officers and men. There was a burnished brass bell that fairly blinded you, and everywhere the brassware was the same, and they received me courteously and asked if there was much night life in Basra. If there was, I had not tasted it myself yet, but managed an exaggerated knowing wink. I returned to my awaiting truck, looking at my dusty, dishevelled khaki drill uniform, and wondered what it must be like to be smart and in the Senior Service. I remember our journeys through the streets of Basra as hair-raising, for the drivers always maintained that you could not forge your way through unless you kept your foot down and your hand on the horn.

CHAPTER 7

Shaibah

HURRICANE AND FLOODS

On Monday 8 May, we were aware that something was different about the camp. Firstly, there was a stronger scent of oil in the air. As the wind started to freshen up, we stood looking at the horizon and it appeared to be one dark line that gradually grew thicker. Then brushwood came swiftly bowling through the camp at a rate of knots, like some cowboy western. At the same time the temperature dropped, from steamy hot to freezing cold. We were then literally hit by hail so large and so fierce that we dived for the shelter of the billet and tried to watch through the window. Some who were caught out in the storm were stung by the weight and size of the stones, and we played marbles with them until they melted. The rain, so heavy and prolonged, sat on the hard concrete-like surface of the camp, and quickly formed into a flood. The MT billet were bailing out as they had lost part of their roof. The airfield tower billet had lost most of its roof. Trees were down by the officers' mess, and our recently built NAAFI bar at poolside was a crumpled wreck; the windbreak wall alongside the tennis courts had partially gone. The floods took some time to subside; one had to paddle everywhere for a while and the free-standing toilet block, some distance from the main billets, had its large receptacle tanks with their chemical and other deposits afloat.

VISITING AIRCRAFT

On the tail of the hurricane came an aircraft, seeking a safe landing. A French medical team in a Junkers 52 who had followed the storm, had to make such a detour it had reduced their fuel range. The airfield ground staff were out lighting a flare path, and were very tired that night. I had the chance the next day to have a close look at the Junkers, with its strangely corrugated and unique body, and its triple engines; one like a bottle stopper stuck on its snout. From time to time, aircraft other than the regular twice-weekly duty Dakotas, and the CO's Anson, adorned the runway. There was a Valetta from time to time, and once a Hawker Sea Fury with its five bladed propellers, which looked quite magnificent. This was flown for the Pakistani Air Force by an ex-RAF pilot. I was at Shaibah to witness the arrival of its first jet aircraft, the beautifully shaped Meteor. The pilot was boasting of its speed, saying that it went so fast, he was in time for breakfast wherever he landed. The Iraqi ground crews in the refuelling vehicles had never seen an aircraft without a propeller, but then neither had I, close up and touchable. There were more Meteors to pass through Shaibah and we were told they were for the Australian Air Force; looked very impressive on the runway.

Visiting aircraft

Loading Dakota

Duty Dakota

Shaibah's very own Avro Anson

Visiting Valetta

Meteors en route for Australia

Refuelling Meteor – pith helmets!

Refuelling Junkers JU 52

French Red Cross – Junkers JU 52

Hawker Sea Fury – Arrives

Ground crew at work

Pilot climbs aboard

Ex-RAF Pilot of Hawker Sea Fury – Pakistan Air Force
is bid farewell by Flight Lieutenant O'Neill

CHAPTER 8

Basra

AND THE SHATT AL ARAB

Visiting Basra, or rather its suburb Asher (because most of Basra was out of bounds to protect our morals), came quite regularly via the camp bus – a Commer coach not on the camp inventory, but acquired and kept in pristine condition by the MT section. One function of this coach was to take the Catholic faithful to Basra once a fortnight and spare seats were for sale. This afforded a chance to get outside the camp, to see a most colourful and interesting place that one could explore forever. The coach always parked opposite a statue of the Lion of Babylon, or so we were told. The lion stands over a prone figure; some called it the Lion of Sheba. This main road housed the more substantial buildings like the post office, with several tables set outside, at which were seated a few scribes awaiting customers who needed their services. Behind the 'Lion' was a bridge over the river that ran into the Shatt al Arab, and teemed with river life and craft of all sizes, including river taxis, booms or small dhows. The large dhows were laden with dates and their crews sitting and sleeping on the dates under tent-like canopies were out on the main Shatt al Arab with the ocean-going freighters.

The other side of the bridge was a new experience of sights, sounds and smells. Over the bridge it ponged a little, but into the bazaar, one soon picked up the pleasant scents of food, for little cafes had their barbecues full of kebabs in sight of the passing trade to tempt the palate. We never ate any of these foods, as we were warned not to by the medics, and certainly not to fall in the river, or be tempted to swim, as you would certainly have to endure all kinds of injections. One little boy selling chapattis grinned and offered his wares to us and they did look quite nice, and full of currants, but on approaching the currants all took flight.

61

The art of bartering was quickly observed. On being told the price of an article, the customer would laugh loudly and offer a quarter, to which the seller would compare the buyer to some base animal and so they would proceed, until a figure of near a third of the original price would be agreed. Both men enjoyed this type of shopping; how much more civilised than picking something off a shelf and paying for it without question or human debate. Young boys would constantly offer their services as guides or porters, when not trying to offer the services of their young sisters to us, but our reply sounded like 'Anae magnoon mahku folus,' which tried to convey that we were mad and had no money.

GAZELLES AND MARSH ARABS

Along the road towards the Shatt al Arab, we frequented a cafe on the riverside to watch the passing date-laden dhows and the more distant freighters, sailing from Basra to the Persian Gulf. This cafe had a pet gazelle that took food from your hand, and was a lovely creature and well-fed, unlike many of the hacks that worked the horse-drawn taxis. On occasions, we had taken refreshment at a place of less repute, which was quite innocent by day, but we had observed the well-veiled upper floor snugs that could tell a tale or two. The lady serving the drinks obviously knew one of our party quite well, and sat on his lap to our embarrassment. Or was it envy? This was 1950, remember, when girls were not so outgoing. On leaving, we stood admiring a flash limousine that had just arrived with two of the most beautiful Oriental girls you could imagine, dressed in silks and adorned with gold. We just gaped and hardly spoke, all with our own fantasies. Basra was magical at times.

An expedition was planned, or, more correctly, we had a boat trip organised, to visit the upper reaches of the Shatt al Arab, to see where the Marsh Arabs dwelt. I remember the sight of cattle standing in the riverside amongst the reeds, being washed down by women and children. We passed under the large metal bridge, taking the road from Basra to Iran; a centre-span of the bridge could be moved to allow the larger and tall-masted, craft-free passage.

NIGHT SCENTS AND OPULENCE

An evening excursion into Asher to sample the delights of their drinking dens commenced quite orderly. A long, pleasant walk offered cooler evening scents of the eucalyptus trees, blending with the cooking smells of many dishes. In some areas, away from the bazaars and main town, were open-air cafes that stretched back to the trees and down to the roadside, about a hundred feet. At their tables, the male adult Arab would be seen drinking arrack, a potent brew that tasted strongly of aniseed, that even when diluted could blow your socks off. They would be playing what looked like dominoes to us, to the sound of many different wireless stations. Taking into account the position of Basra on the map, the radio covered both Iraqi, Iranian, Kuwaiti, Saudi and Indian music. This was accompanied by the bull frogs and a cricket chorus from the watery backwoods. We continued past some high class properties on the waterside, rich businessmen and oil tycoons with floodlit swimming pools and see-through opulence, sat drinking their martinis and ice.

BELLY DANCING AND GYPPY TUMMY

Coming to our less exotic bar, we passed the entrance and had to pay about 250 fils, or purchase a bottle of the house wine. The latter we did on sage advice from the more experienced amongst our party, and promptly gave the wine to our nearest tables, thus gaining some warm approval of the locals. Then we produced bottles of beer brought with us as canned beers were not yet available. The floor show consisted of musicians playing endless twanging music most of the time, but this music can get under your skin. I still get goose bumps on hearing it, even 50 years on. Was I really there? There was a change of tempo, the natives were restless, it was belly-dance time. Our bromide levels were diluted with beer and we arose with expectation. But a rather plump, half-veiled and much-covered dancing lady of mature years sang and danced for us.

We resumed our drinking, but one amongst our crew had developed a severe attack of gyppy tummy and did not find the toilets to his liking, as an old woman had come in to his cubicle quite ignoring him, looking for cigarette butts. He desperately wanted home, so we decided to book two taxis, one to take half the party to some dubious area, and the other to take us back to Shaibah. However, our taxi had only been going a few miles when it turned into an alley of very high walls and stopped at the end, the driver holding out his hand for payment. We quickly realised that the lad who booked the taxi thought we should have the same education that they were about to experience, and had ordered both taxis for the red light district of Basra. This was a place severely out of bounds, and the RAF police patrolled every weekend and reeled in quite a few, including one lad who was brought back to camp with some lady's unmentionables on his head, and very little of his own clothing. This was as close as I ever came to the fleshpots of the Middle East, trust me! The driver was eventually persuaded to drive the other twenty-odd miles in the desert dark of the early hours of the morning, and get us back to camp.

Asher – 'The Lion of Babylon'

Les, Charlie, Jim and the Commer Bus

Asher – Post Office and scribes

Asher – horse-drawn taxi

Ship and dhows at anchor

Asher – Mosque and minaret

Asher – Shatt al Arab

Riverside Café – Gazelle and laden dhow

Heading up-river

Steamships on the Shatt al Arab

Dhow at anchor

River ferry

Sailing through

Bridge to the markets of Asher

Riverside traders and merchants

Asher – river life

Riverside warehouses

Asher – hardware souk

Chapatti sellers

Fruit and vegetable market

Cafe with balconies

Pleasant riverside shade

Mealtime in Basra

Back alley

Mosque and warehouse

CHAPTER 9

Shaibah Animals

DOGS – WHISKY AND HOMER

We had two resident dogs on camp. One was a small white highland terrier of sorts, usually called Whisky, as he looked like one half of the pair of dogs on a 'Black and White' whisky bottle. By some, he was called Jock and to others Harry; he answered to all, but he was the only dog that I have known with a race prejudice, for levies and Arab workers would be barked out of sight. Homer was mostly a mongrel with a touch of wild piard and quickly transferred his affections to a new airman when one of his keepers got posted, and regularly deposited small dead rodents at the side of his keeper's bed. The sand lizards fascinated him, and he would chase them endlessly and pounce, to have their tail still wriggling under his paw whilst the detached body ran away to grow another one. Homer, more than Whisky, would attach himself to anyone with time on their hands. He would accompany us on our rides inside the camp, and frequented the stable area and the poolside, and one thing for sure, these dogs never wanted for company.

Homer

HORSES – BLONDIE, PETER AND BILL

There were three horses stabled at the rear of the main camp, near to the pig sties, and had a stable yard that boasted of some small trees, under which Hamad's pigeon boxes took some shade. He lovingly tended them when not looking after the horses. Jim Forte introduced me to the pleasures of horse riding and throughout my stay, I rode out with him as often as we could afford, although the cost of riding was not that expensive. By making ourselves useful to Hamad, we got lots of free rides, as due to the terrain of hard sand and roads, with no grassy paddocks for them to gallop freely, he liked them to be walked, or lightly ridden, near the stables to keep them fit.

Jim was less cautious and goaded me to join in some more adventurous trips outside the camp. We took it in turn to ride Peter, who Hamad assured us was trained as a polo pony. He did move in quick bursts from time to time and he was the most comfortable to ride. Then there was Bill, who could have been trained as a mule, for although great when you got him going, was very stubborn at times. Mainly on leaving the stable yard, but on returning from a mile out, he would fairly bolt home.

Blondie, so called for he had a light golden coat with a blonde mane, was bred for racing we were assured, and he could have been. Sadly, he was severely lame, and although Hamad's bandages and bathing did improve him for a while, some months later he was put down. Jim and I could not bear to be within a mile of the deed, but did return at night to see him buried; we both had walked or trotted him around the camp, but had never really ridden Blondie.

The nearest that I got to a ride on Blondie was when Hamad asked me to give him a good workout, as he was becoming fractious in his stall. I could see what he meant; he was actually kicking his stallion appendage that swung way down, for he was a young horse, lacking a mate, and bored with inactivity. I nervously offered to ride him, in the cooler late afternoon if he was calmer. With a little trepidation, I eventually took Blondie for a walk, within the confines of the main camp, enjoying very much the passing attention we got from all those around who were glad to see Blondie about again. We proceeded towards the main gate, passing the scrap and kerosene compounds, when an engine sounded its whistle and immediately my ride became electric. I daren't dismount, for he was raring to do a bolt, and I would not have been able to hold him. Fortunately, an Arab civilian on his way home had the presence of mind to hold his head for me and slowly walk him to the gate, where we both calmed down. Just outside the gate, we walked around until the train had gone, and so slowly returned to the stables, whereupon I breathed a sigh of relief. Later walks on Blondie were in the empty, quiet side of the camp.

RIDING OUT

One of our trips outside was to explore the area to the rear of the camp, which took us through disused billets that were half submerged and had concrete entrances that led down a few steps, more like the barracks of the Foreign Legion forts. Picking our way through broken roadways, covered with windswept desert bric-a-brac, loose pieces of barbed wire were our main worry. Passing some old buildings with doors and windows broken or missing, like a ghost town in the Mexican outback, we came to the gate, and the Baluchi guards waved us through. The desert was vast, and as someone once said on approaching Alice Springs in Australia, just miles and miles of bugger all. It was twenty-odd miles to the borders of Kuwait and now sadly remembered as the killing road from Kuwait. But this was 1950 and such horrors were not dreamt of, and we were two lowly airmen out for a ride. We passed an experimental fenced-off area, in which the Iraqis were growing all kinds of plants. There must have been a well somewhere in its midst, or a very long pipeline. This would not have surprised me, for Iraq has many thousands of miles of pipeline and on some rides, we used large oil pipes that stood some feet above ground to guide our course and our safe return. We eventually came to habitation and on the fringes, gingerly walked among the palms and furrowed sandy soil, which was so much easier to ride on. We had a little canter, no sign of humans, but suddenly the sounds of dogs growing louder. I was first to suggest we go no further and Jim reluctantly agreed. It was, as I pointed out, best not to risk us having to gallop the horses and chance some injury; Hamad would not want another lame horse. Hamad's parting shot was, 'Do not let them gallop!' – directed more at Jim than I – so on returning, Jim and I got off our mounts and walked to let them cool down after a little canter outside the camp. But on remounting and in sight of the stables, Bill took us at a gallop anyway, right into his stall before you could dismount. It was a case of putting your head well down, or hit the door frame of the stable, and with Hamad shouting, 'You've galloped them,' Jim replied 'No, they did it all on their own.'

SHAIBAH'S DOGS

Homer – Charlie, Ron and Ginger

Whisky – Dave, Charlie and Don

THE STABLES

Homer and Jim

Peter and I

Blondie and Jim

Stables, Hamad and his pigeons

Blondie and Jim

Blondie and I

Peter and Jim

Outside camp

Bill and I – riding out of camp

Bedouin camp

Zubair

OIL RIGS

Another memorable ride out of camp was via the main gate, and on passing some Bedouin encampment, quite near to this front gate, we were tempted to see if we could get a camel ride. But all sorts of silly tales about catching some unmentionable diseases from them put us off. Instead, we carried on to our main quest – visiting one of the oil rigs within sight of the camp, and part of the Zubair oilfield. We nearly didn't make it, as Peter, my mount, lunged to one side, almost shipping me, as something had frightened him. Jim thought he saw a snake, but it could have been any creature. We did not hang around, letting our horses ride away from the spot. We trotted on and were received warmly by the rig crew, who were of all nationalities, including some Americans. They offered us their hospitality of cookies and coffee, whilst finding a shady spot for the horses that they fussed over, enjoying the diversion. They gave us a tour of the rig and I noticed how brightly painted all of their trucks were; yellows and orange colours stood out, presumably for spotting them in the flat brown landscape.

The Iraqi crew of rig workers were busily attaching a pipe at the head, with huge clamps swinging into place and water splashing around. It was mid-afternoon and very hot, and they all looked soaked in sweat. 'Would you like to go up the rig?' I thought it nice of them to ask. Even on good, hot, sunny days in southern Iraq, the wind can blow mighty fierce and this day was no exception. As soon as my foot hit the metal rung of the awaiting ladder to the sky, I could feel the vibrations, and only a sense of bravado made me climb rapidly to a platform halfway up the rig. Fortunately, the ladder had guard bands around it, but my vertigo thoughts were there. Clutching a handrail on the platform and almost to the top of the stacked pipes that rattled and clanged against the rig, I waved below, then looked up at the tapering tower above, as if to climb to the top. But I bandaged my pride and quivered down to safe terra firma. I was too busy with my own thoughts and cannot recall if Jim made it to the top. Bidding farewell to our hosts, we set off back to the ranch house for tea.

Zubair oil rig

Iraqi oil rig crew – 19-year-old foreman in beret

CHAPTER 10

Shaibah

BOMB DISPOSALS

Shaibah had a surfeit of out of date bangers; I think they were 30lb shells or bombs. At intervals, selected airmen were to find themselves seconded to the armoury and, in three-tonners, headed out to the ammunition dump. This underground area was huge and stacked with neat piles of varied missiles in mini pyramids that were no longer wanted. All we had to do was load some shells into neat rows on the floor of the truck and sit on the wheel arches inside with our feet resting on the bangers, whilst we then rattled along out of camp to a designated detonation site.

Once there, we again had to carry these shells, cradled like newborn babes, to a series of trenches, dug out and awaiting their arrival. They were laid in neat rows of 30 at a time and I cannot remember the full total. When our carrying tasks were completed, the truck deposited the officer in charge of disposal, and his crew, at a concrete lookout post. Then they dropped us airmen, in pairs, at the other three corners of the square, all with a red and a green flag, and a trestle-table for protection against shrapnel. We sat there for ages, awaiting the bomb disposal squad to set the gun-cotton and to detonate the bombs. While waiting, we had to ensure that no humans or livestock wandered into the square. On one occasion, we had cause to raise our red flag on sighting an Arab and his flock of sheep very close, but when warned away he replied, 'I have read standing orders, sir, and I like to watch.' Obviously an off duty civilian worker.

Finally, all was clear and a three-minute signal was given by the look-out. All green flags were waving, followed by a very long three minutes, then a quiet thud, followed by an almighty bang, and whistling that I had not heard since the Birmingham air raids. Some bits of shrapnel sailed past us and one hit the table. We then examined the table more closely to see it was pitted with numerous direct hits. 'Would it not be possible to move the tables out a bit more, sir?' we asked. 'What?! And miss all the fun?' was the reply. 'Anyway,' he added, 'I wouldn't be able to see the colour of your little flags, would I?'

HOSEPIPES AND STEN GUNS

Another RAF requirement was a corporate understanding of fire drill, and we were marshalled out on the hottest and sweatiest of days to run the hoses to and from the fire hydrants and the fire tender. Taking it in turns to unroll and manhandle these heavy, incredibly self-willed pipes, we were to deliver a water jet in the right direction, at an imaginary fire, and not at our instructors. At the rear of the fire drill area stood the firing range, where all duty clerks were to report for Sten gun practice. This was after a Duty Officer had discovered that none of us had ever actually seen one fired, let alone handled and fired one. On the range, we had a standing-man target and if you started firing low at eight o'clock, the momentum carried your spray of shots through the target, finishing about two o'clock skywards. This we enjoyed doing so much they soon stopped it, saying we were now proficient enough. This was in contrast to my Padgate 303 rifle range work, carried out when a sore throat and nasty headache rendered every bang a torture, and every shot a failure. Not as good as at the Onion Fair in Aston, where I could at least manage to down a tin elephant or hippo.

HAPLESS PIGS

Swine fever ceased our supply of fresh pork and gave me my most unpleasant task to date, as I, along with other 'volunteers', had to help round up the pigs for slaughter. This was done quite quickly and as humanely as possible, but by the knife, in what had until then been the piggery. Each one went in one door and the carcass out the other, fairly quickly, that is except for the old sow, which flew out of the door I was next to. In her last moments, when my selfish, immediate thoughts were not to get blood all over my socks and shoes, she reached the fence and there promptly expired. I relate this short, sad tale because it was another experience in service life that moved me greatly; fortunately, our services were not required for the disposal of the remains of these hapless pigs.

INTRODUCED TO CURRY

Our meals on the whole were fair, but the meat lacked a little something, and it was usually so chewy and tough we thought it must be camel. We also had a dehydrated powder that could be resurrected to resemble mashed potato; however, the resident chef had a desire to improve its looks and turned out formations of little twisted dollops. These quickly dried out, to leave a surface of sharp edges, hiding a khaki inside like wet cardboard. The Arab assistants in the cookhouse had a much more interesting fare, as every day their pot of curry aroused the taste buds and the cooks themselves did partake of it, so I was quickly converted. I nearly made a big mistake on my first meal in the mess hall, seeing a very dark-tanned man with a shaven head serving the meals. I thought him one of Allah's chosen, only to find that he had a broad north country accent. There was a change of chef soon after, who did wonders with the food. It soon became so good that the officers' mess tried to second his services and, after much objection, finally succeeded.

LANCASHIRE HOTPOT AND TOMBOLA

Our NAAFI manager had a very pleasant tradition of inviting around six airmen to join him in a meal each month. This consisted of a very large Lancashire hotpot with wine, beer and hours of conversation, which made a pleasant change from the usual fare of double egg and chips (not being greedy) for Shaibah eggs were so very small. Tombola night, housey-housey or lotto (now called bingo) was held on pay day, and the usual caller's name was Eddie. He also answered to the name of PMG, being our camp's resident 'Postmaster General'. Pay day, or as Shaibah airmen would say, 'The day the golden eagle shits,' became fortnightly, as did tombola. There was a roll-over jackpot called a snowball, which had accumulated to equal many weeks' pay and no one was about to miss this chance, as all had contributed to it over many weeks. The morning of the great tombola, I met a newcomer while shaving. He had come up from Sharjah and was running down our camp, saying, 'What the hell is there to do here?' So I said, 'Well, there's tombola tonight, with a big rollover snowball.' The lucky newcomer won it.

The NAAFI had two full-size snooker tables and this room was a delightful retreat, especially in the heat of the day, to escape into its dark, deliciously cool atmosphere and pot a few. On those evenings that funds provided (usually on pay days), the drinking started inside the NAAFI, with double egg and chips. Then the party progressed to the tables outside the NAAFI, with large bottles of ale, safely stored in the centre of the table, the dead ones relegated underneath. We would talk, tell jokes and sing bawdy songs under a bat-filled sky, with occasional trips to the loo, or a walk around the floodlit pool. Here, a late bather may be still swimming at two in the morning; it was that kind of camp. One sergeant, who was not a good swimmer, was blissfully afloat on a small wooden raft after an evening of merriment and had to be brought to safety. 'I'm unshinkable,' he was saying.

Shaibah

General view from hangars

Camp cinema and theatre

Poolside

Poolside sandy lawn

Diving board or sunbed

Poolside – soft drinks bar

Pool sprinklers at work

Cooling off   *Charlie, Geordie and Mac*

CHAPTER 11

Shaibah

POOL AND SKINNY-DIPPING

I learned to swim at Shaibah, with the aid of a smooth, solid wooden raft. This was large enough for two or three to sit astride whilst repelling the opposing team, swimming under or straight at the raft, grabbing your legs or hands. The aim was to make the length of the pool using only one's hands as paddles with at least one still aboard. This raft could be used to hold and push in front of you to practice your leg movements when learning to swim. But my main tutor was a half-inflated one-man dinghy, acting as superb water wings. I had attained the one-width proficiency when I kicked off fiercely to do a width, only to have leg cramp a short way across. I panicked and felt myself sinking down, down, and on touching bottom, had the sense to kick up. I must only have been in about ten feet of water and could see the diving boards above me. I took a gulp of air and went down again. Why I did not shout, or try to swim when up for air, I do not know, but I bobbed up and down before someone on the raft grabbed me and said, 'I thought you were playing some sort of game!' After that, I learned to float on my back in case it happened again. The pool was well-used and had a grass-covered area on one side, with a NAAFI soft drinks bar where one crashed out to dry in the sun. The one end of the pool had a footbath and shower, and it was common for airmen to come off duty, hot and sweaty, take a shower and dive in, as bathers were not obligatory. On occasion the, officers would invite civilians from Basra, some probably from the oil business, to partake of the camp's amenities, such as the pool and cinema. When this occurred, we had to warn the swimmers to dress up a notch, but wickedly did not warn one bronzed Adonis who liked to take his time sunbathing on the high board. Quite unaware of the visitors, he gracefully executed his dive starkers, and surfaced to find the pool filling up with young mothers and their offspring, all enjoying his embarrassment.

94

WATER BABIES AND FROGS

Some babies that came, barely toddlers, were already able to swim, and put us late starters to shame. The pool soon filled up with weekend swimmers, all ogling the lovely ladies, which was a rare chance not to be missed. The concrete flagstones surrounding the pool became unbearably hot in the course of the day and had to be continuously hosed down by a civilian. He also scooped up the dead mosquitoes and horseflies from the pool, and put them in the gutter around the flagstones. We would watch, fascinated, as the colonies of small ants battled with the big ants to see who would drag the spoils away. Later, frogs (or they may have been toads) were introduced into the pool and helped keep it clean, but it's quite comical to have a frog swimming alongside you, taking care not to open one's mouth too wide. It was prudent to look in the footbath tray to ensure that no water-seeking scorpion had dropped in by accident. The pool was equipped with water jets from each side that formed two arches of water, and in the noonday sun, they were pleasant to swim under.

CINEMA AND 'THE THIEF OF BAGHDAD'

The cinema shows were mainly weekly affairs and were either open air or indoor, depending on the weather. Civilian workers and other invited guests also came, and language had to be restrained when ladies were present. I can remember two films that graced our screen. The first was Doris Day in *It's Magic*, which was popular with the lads. But when its title certificate showed the American version called *Romance on the High Seas*, the cinema erupted, thinking we had been cheated. But then the voice of Doris Day singing 'It's Magic' restored calm. The second film was Sabu's *Thief of Baghdad*, which was a delight for all the assembled Arabs, many with young children, who were ecstatic every time Baghdad or Basra was named. They shouted abuse at Conrad Veidt as he called on the wind to help him shipwreck our hero. The performances were enhanced by bags of hot, roasted peanuts, purchased from a vendor outside the cinema, and downing liquor from bottles of all kinds, purchased at the NAAFI. However, if the bottles got shook up and were cold from the ice box, unopened and in the heat they would explode like bombs. The outdoor screen would also acquire lizards, walking up an actor's face, and shadows thrown by our resident bats on the wing.

CHAPTER 12

Shaibah

SICK BAY

I awoke early one morning and felt unwell. I was very feverish and had a severe pain in my chest on breathing in, and thought, here comes my old friend pneumonia again. I told my mates and reported to sick bay, where the Medical Officer quickly got me into a ward. There were three others in there with varying ailments, and I was thoroughly examined and prescribed penicillin. The medical orderly, about my age, came in with a small kidney bowl, complete with a syringe and file of penicillin. He duly loaded his missile and advanced upon me. I bravely offered my arm, but he declined, saying, 'You've to have it in your bum, turn over.' This I did. He said, 'If you don't relax it may ache afterwards.' He then gave me a sharp smack on my buttock and pressed home the needle. 'It's supposed to relax the muscles,' he said, fearing I might misinterpret his slap as a sign of affection. After a while, and a few slaps later, I began to feel loads better and said as much to my new chums, who cautioned me not to be too anxious to get well. 'It's cushy in here,' they told me, 'and the orderlies are great, they get our food for us, and some bottles of beer they smuggle in make it OK.' I need not have worried, for the Medical Officer was not expecting me to be fit for at least a week as, taking my history into account, he thought I had bronchial pneumonia. He would require an x-ray before releasing me, so I settled for the idle life and read a lot, just as I used to as a lad when recovering from illness.

My most favourite book was *Robinson Crusoe*, which I read many times. Eventually, the day came for my x-ray – not at camp, for unlike Habbaniya, this was not a hospital, only a sick bay with no x-ray facilities. I was taken some twenty miles to Basra Hospital and lined up with the Arabs for photo-call. It was very interesting, but I had no signs to read to pass the time as, thoughtlessly, they were mostly in Arabic.

Several days later, the MO checked me over and said, 'If you feel well enough, I shall let you go, as the x-rays from the hospital were not of your chest and I don't want you to go through it all again.'

WILLIE'S UNWELL

The only other time that I was to trouble the Medical Officer came about through the sheer naivety of a nineteen-year-old airman, namely me. I had, on taking a shower, noticed a slight smear of blood on my towel and was shaken to find that it emanated from the end of my willy. Quickly drying myself, I retired to the privacy of a toilet, and stared hard and long as the pinpricks of blood returned. I wanted a doctor, but perhaps it would be gone by tomorrow. It had not, so once more, with much trepidation, I put myself on sick parade and awaited my time to see the MO. I had heard that all manner of diseases could be caught from lavatory seats, and not believed it, but something was amiss. I thought I was for the dreaded willy needle treatment at Habbaniya hospital.

How shall I put it to the MO? And what do I call it? This was 1950 and such things were not openly spoken of or discussed, and certainly not in medical terms which seemed even ruder to say than the common slang. So I decided to call it dick.

'So, let's have a look at Dick. How long since your last intercourse?'

I felt inadequate and said, 'I haven't.'

'What, never?' he said.

'No, never,' said I.

Then after a quick shufti he said, 'It's a common problem out here, you have an infection due to sand irritation. Give this prescription to the orderly; he will give you some ointment.'

I walked out a much happier little airman.

MOBILE DENTAL UNIT

I have an ongoing dislike of the dentist's chair, from my first visit to the dental centre that existed in Moseley. In this place, frightened children shuffled along benches until they reached their turn for a seat in one of a row of high black chairs and received a painful jaw stretcher, just prior to a rubbery mask obliterating their mind. On awaking, a big solid nurse would thump you, telling you to stop that crying even before you were awake enough to spit blood into the small awaiting basin. So when Jim and I met the visiting Dental Officer, who was out riding Peter, on asking us where the best riding was to be had, I could not have been more helpful, as I had to see him the next day and wanted some insurance or Brownie points. He was very tall in the saddle, and seemed even taller as he towered over me in the chair. Already sweating in the heat of the afternoon, I braced myself as he prodded and poked, and felt about one of my front teeth. Every prod hit my eyeball with the pain. He drew back and said, 'I'll do my best to save this one, bear with me.' I could see some of the dental orderlies observing the torture as his drill started to penetrate into the centre of the rotten tooth. With a clockwise movement he found all my nerves well awake. Down he went and I followed; up, up and I followed. He did not seem to mind me gasping in pain one bit, and finally he seemed content. He bunged the 'hole with a tooth' full of cement and I staggered out into the blazing sun, dripping wet. I should point out, we had no pain-killing injections for dental work. My dentist, many years later and about to separate me from my faithful molar, remarked that it was a pity that the filling had gone yellow as it was still rock solid. 'It must have had too much sand in the mix,' I said, but that quip was understood by me and my tooth alone.

SAND AND SHIT STORMS

At certain times of the year, the wind was relentless and prevailed for three or four days at a time. So fierce was it, that the sand and dust forced itself into every crevice and matted your hairs, both top and bottom when in shorts. It got behind your sunglasses and into the corners of your eyes, up your nose, lodged in your ears and stuck to your sweat like sugar on a jam doughnut. To wipe the sweat off your brow felt like a caress of sandpaper, and toilet rolls had the quality of emery paper. The wind forced you to walk headfirst into it at an angle, and to lean back when it was behind you. To open your mouth meant gritty teeth. We must have swallowed a bucketful. The showers and the pool helped, but you still had to fight your way through it on the way back.

Baghdad – midday

Tigris – South with solitary coracle

Tigris – North – Old City and minarets

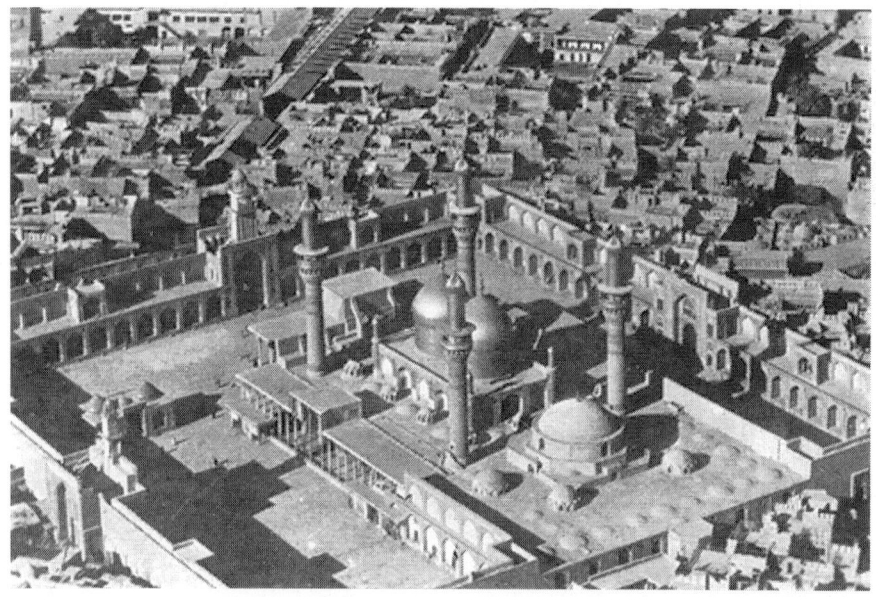

Baghdad – Golden Palace

Baghdad and Mosul

Hostelry palms

Mosul – view from RAF camp

Mosul

Part of the 15cwt truck convoy

Jim at rear of truck – Mosul

Northern Iraq

Convoy and mules on mountain pass

Kurdish guard

Hill village near Dohuk

The 'Seven Sisters' climb

CHAPTER 13

Ser–Amadia

BASRA TO BAGHDAD

On Thursday 24 August 1950, I began my first leave abroad. This was to be two weeks in Kurdistan at the RAF rest and leave camp of Ser-Amadia, just south of the Turkish frontier. It required two train journeys of about 550 miles, then by 15cwt trucks for another 60 miles, and finally by mule to a height of 6,000 feet.

The first part of our journey commenced at Basra railway station, from where our party of about ten travelled up to Baghdad. I enjoyed this trip even more than my first on coming south, as I had spent eight months at Shaibah, and this was the first time that I had travelled the line for pleasure only, and with companions who were not strangers. Someone had brought a bottle of arrack to try and, upon obtaining the usual jug of iced water from the attendant, we passed the brew around. Being very thirsty, I took a good swig and have never experienced such an explosion before or since. It felt like my head was expanding outwards. Gradually, my vision returned. Most of us had felt a similar reaction, so it was sips from then on, and we did have a very merry trip. Next morning at Baghdad, we were taken to some kind of hostelry to spend the night, which gave me a chance to see the fabled city. I visited a museum with models and artefacts of Ur of the Chaldees, and of Babylon and the hanging gardens. It was midday and the streets were quiet, with all at meals or siesta, for only mad dogs and Englishmen were abroad. I visited a large bookshop and obtained a copy of *A Thousand and One Nights* to send home to my younger brother, David. I thought it the most appropriate one. We then walked over a long, wide bridge spanning the Tigris, and save for an Arab in a coracle sculling downstream, the river seemed empty. There was no time to see the Palace, so I purchased an aerial view photo, to see what it looked like. Our short stay was most pleasant and the hostelry had a covered walkway around an inner garden, which was tranquil and cool. Outside the front entrance, a few date palms helped to set the scene. We sat after our meal for a long conversation with the reverend gentleman in charge, telling us over iced drinks a little about life in Baghdad.

BAGHDAD TO MOSUL

Our party was taken to Baghdad station to join up with the leave-takers from Habbaniya. They were a larger party, but we did not travel together and they were at the other end of the train. It was suggested they must have WAAF nurses with them and could not trust the Shaibah lads to behave like proper gentlemen, but we never saw any trace of them. Once again, we travelled by rail to new territory and arrived at Mosul on Sunday morning, 27 August 1950, where we were taken to the RAF camp for refreshment and rest, while awaiting our transport for the next stage of our journey. Whilst waiting, we could observe from a distance the minaret in Mosul and were told that this leaned like the tower of Pisa, but we did not get near enough to verify. At last our transport was ready, in the shape of a convoy of smart-looking 15cwt trucks, which, once loaded, headed back into Mosul. We were on our way to the mountains of the Kurds.

MOSUL TO BABAIDI

On leaving Mosul, the convoy made its way north for about 40 miles before turning right to Dohuk, where we took a break for refreshments. Here, we were flanked on one side by flat-roofed dwellings in the foot-hills of the mountains, and on the other side by the valley. Soon, we were climbing hairpin roads, then a zigzag of roads named the seven sisters by our drivers. The narrow passes through the hills were barely wide enough for two-way traffic at many places. These were full of horse or mule transport with Kurds; many sporting old long muskets on their backs, and large curved knives in their belts, with bandoleers of firepower across their chests. 'It's the second Khyber Pass,' we thought, little knowing how these areas would, in a later time, once more erupt with internal religious fighting. Some 30-odd miles from Dohuk, we turned in to a transit stage post called Babaidi, to make acquaintance with our next means of transportation.

BABAIDI TO SER-AMADIA

Mules come in all shapes and sizes, and I was looking for a big one to suit my long legs. However, fate decreed that the artful dodger of the Khyber Pass, namely Bobo the muleteer, had already adopted me and placed my kit on one mule, and me on another. The Postmaster General was insisting that he would walk up, rather than burden a mule with his weight. He was stocky, and not a fat person, but obviously felt sorry for any creature about to take his weight. Each muleteer had several mules in his charge, with one carrying luggage only. The mule train thus organised, we were checked off the list. In small groups, we crossed the road and into a thicket. Following a thin trail along a mountain stream, then onward and upward, the path gave way to a pile of well-worn stony rubble that masqueraded as a path; the mules had to reach full length to stride over boulders to obtain the next foothold. We were told that we had to climb some thousand feet or more to the camp. After a short while, we came to a suitable spot to let the mules rest. We were exhausted, too, with the effort of staying aboard these tough and wiry steeds at an angle with your nose up the mule's ear hole. Eddie, the PMG, came manfully struggling up and, absolutely exhausted, finally agreed to ride his mule. We had all been impressed by these animals, with their strength and almost goat-like abilities whilst carrying our weight. At the head of the ravine, the pathway began to be less steep and soon we were out in more open ground, with a track that you could see winding its way up the side of a mountain slope. Along this, we progressed slowly, with a huge rolling slope down to our right, which grew further to fall as the further up we went. Our steeds delivered us, at last, to the rest and leave camp of Ser-Amadia, some 6,000 feet above sea level.

Ser-Amadia

Arriving at Ser-Amadia

RAF Rest and Leave Camp – Ser-Amadia

Roy signals to me at camp

My trusty pit

Roy scales the heights

Self, Roy, George, Norman, Reg, Don and Eddie

Reg out for an early walk

The two campsites

On the way to Black Rock Springs – children watch

Black Rock Springs

Resting on way down

Roy admires the view

Black Rock Valley

Black Rock Spring

CHAPTER 14

Ser–Amadia

LIFE OF LEISURE

This was the life; no work for a couple of weeks, due for demob on 14 December, and I would be home well before Christmas. I would be packing up my old kit bag for Blighty in about four months; what a full eighteen months this would have been. There was not a lot to explore on the camp; it contained all the necessary amenities with a mess tent, a NAAFI tent, a toilet tent and a washhouse tent. A shack of some kind that was the cookhouse and hundreds of guy ropes to be avoided. The weather was a lot cooler than down at Shaibah, for during our leave, Shaibah had topped 120 degrees and when we had left there it was approaching 110 degrees. The temperature of a mere 80 degrees seemed perfect. There were cinema shows on special nights, outdoor of course. I remember that on one occasion our group had decided to watch from a distance, up the mountain side, out of sound. With our beer or mineral bottles lined up, we enjoyed the lovely soft coolness of the evening, with a star-filled sky above us. Partway down the hill, the screen showed the huge heads of film stars, but to us the stars off-screen, and the mountains that stretched out to Turkey, were of more interest.

In the heat of the day, it was possible to have trouble with wasps of the north Iraqi Kurdish variety, which were built like gunships and bigger than I have seen elsewhere. On one particular day, they seemed to be very active and the mess tent was alive with them, particularly around the bread, jam and butter table. This was covered with a mesh that seemed to have been put there to keep us out and the wasps in. Not wanting a wasp buttie, I grabbed the main meal, a mug of tea, and ran back to the safety of my tent, dived in and fastened up the flap. Then I spent a few minutes dispatching the ones that had followed me. For added protection, I crawled under the mosquito net that adorned my bed and finally enjoyed the meal.

BLACK ROCK SPRINGS

On Tuesday 29 August, we decided on a modest trek to Black Rock Springs, a lovely valley with more trees than we had seen for a while, including poplars and walnut trees. The approach to this valley had long stretches of twisted smaller trees; perhaps these were also walnuts. I recall the RAF levy coming on the walk with us, saying that there were brown bears in this region, therefore a levy guide with a rifle was useful. I think, however, the guide was there to make sure we did not stray into Turkey by mistake. Soon afterwards, a crashing sound descended towards us and we waited in excitement. Was it a bear? No, it was a strapping youth with a stave, running downhill at speed, and striking trees as he went. We stood back amazed. It must either be a local pastime, or he's very late for work. A few days later we were told that a levy had shot at a bear two miles off camp to keep it away. On starting our journey, we had passed some very young girls standing on top of massive boulders, observing our passing with quiet dignity, but did not respond to our waves of greeting and just watched us out of sight.

Black Rock Springs, we were assured, figured in biblical references, but then most places in Iraq could claim the same. It was, however, a place of beauty with trees and shade, and cascading out of the rocks a most refreshingly ice cold stream of water that we both enjoyed drinking and washing our tired, sweaty feet in. We were told that the leave camp had once faced in a different direction, but some hill tribesmen had taken potshots at the tents from a distance, presumably for practice or fun. We were assured that it had not occurred since its relocation. 'Not yet, anyway,' quipped the line-shooting guardians of the leave camp.

DOWN TO SULAVI

We had prepared on Wednesday for a big mule trek the following day, and the Mess Sergeant was to give us some pack rations. The day was spent organising our party and ordering the mules for an early start, ensuring that Bobo would again provide my steed. Thursday 31 August began one giant of a day; a cool early morning start just after breakfast, loaded with some food and my water bottle full of water. Some had foolishly taken beer. Finally mounted, our party of Shaibah wallahs slowly headed downwards towards the ravine, and Sulavi, preceded by a party of local Kurdish men women and children with their mules, heading in the same direction. They were probably bearing the fruits of their labours, as hill farmers, for sale or barter at Sulavi. There is a different technique for descending a steep hillside by mule, as we were doing in reverse the trip up from Babaidi, but in another ravine, joining the same road further round at Sulavi. This time our stirrups were nearer the mule's ears as we lay backwards. However, for most of the downward journey, we were able to walk alongside our mounts, exercising our leg muscles for a change. Partway down the ravine, we stopped for a rest and a drink from our bottles (and, of course, a cigarette) in a dark shallow cave that Bobo had recommended to us. The cave was so cool, and we had already been on the trail almost two hours. Those with beer found it quite flat and tepid and wished that they had brought water. In another hour, we had reached the back of Sulavi, and picked our way between the buildings and on to the road. At the very first roadside cafe, the rest of our party was already tucking into grapes and sipping hot tea or cold lemonade, and soon we joined them. We stayed some time as the lads were cooling the mules down, ready for a big climb ahead.

Early morning

Mules in camp

Family of Kurds head for Sulavi

Down the ravine

Down the ravine

Bobo's cave

Sulavi

Sulavi dwellings

Bobo brings his mules into Sulavi

George, Norman and Ernest

Roy and I cool off

Main mountain road

Sulavi

Amadia

Valley and Amadia

Reg, Roy, Don, Norman, Ernest and Eddie

Amadia from Sulavi

High up in the town of Amadia

Sulavi and up to camp

George, Don, Norman, Reg and I return to Sulavi

Homeward bound at the head of the ravine

Family of Kurds head for Sulavi

Family of Kurds head for Sulavi

UP TO AMADIA

We could see our objective rising from the valley floor, hundreds of feet higher than we were on the road. To reach it, we had to go some distance along the road and around a bend to the other side. Here, a smaller road descended to the foot of the valley before climbing to the summit of the hill on which the table top fortress town of Amadia stood. After some considerable puffing and panting, we all reached this impressive town, but found the streets empty. Presumably we had hit siesta time. There was, I recall, a mosque and minaret, but we saw no shops or cafes – almost monastic. Years later it was reported that this town had been bombed, and the church and library were hit. Valuable treasures of gold, books and manuscripts were removed; some were auctioned in Mosul and others in Dohuk. On reading this, it saddened me to think that such a peaceful and unique town should be so disturbed. Our photos taken, we then had to wend our way back to Sulavi for more refreshments, before the long hard slog up the ravine to Bobo's cave. Finally, up the steep path, we reached the paddock of the leave camp. Then, unsaddling our mounts that had borne us for many long hours on this very physical and interesting day, we washed away the dust of our trek and ate heartily that night. When comparing Bobo to the artful dodger, I referred to his streetwise ability, for he was a big lad compared to the other mule handlers. With a very thick shock of black hair and two huge brown eyes arched by thick bushy eyebrows, he was never worried, and kept his mules and riders in check. He always looked as if he really loved his work, and was ever eager to show his mountains to us. The muleteers walked, ran and scrambled their way on foot, rarely riding their mules, and their stamina was most impressive.

CHAPTER 15

Ser-Amadia

SUNSTROKE AND SIX MONTHS

We had a few days' rest from long rides to enable the bum and foot blisters to heal; we then re-visited Black Rock Springs for a gentle stroll, and once more enjoyed it very much. It was a very hot day, and we had been glad to avail ourselves of the cool spring waters. On heading back, I removed my sweat-soaked shirt and tied it around my waist, but the upward climb back to camp laid my neck and back open to the glare of the sun. Only later, as I felt heady did I wrap my shirt around my neck. Alas! It was too late. I had my meal, but felt unwell and retired to my little bunk, and sleep. Awaking, I found that I had a thumping head and felt nauseated. My mates were all for the medics, but I said, 'Give me a day first; I don't want to be put on a charge for abuse of my health.' Roy and Don went for a short walk of a couple of miles, and from a high vantage point tried to signal me. But without any binoculars and with my sore eyes I never saw them, so they took photos to prove the point. Whilst languishing in my pit, just having a shave at about twelve noon, I had a visit from an officer making his rounds, seeing that everything was tickety-boo. I said that we were having a very good time, but that yesterday I must have done a little too much, or had too much to drink, and was feeling the effects. He said, 'That's what leave camps are all about.' Then, almost as an afterthought he said, 'Oh! By the way, due to the international unrest, the National Service lads have got to do an extra six months.'

He must have seen my jaw hit the floor, and said, 'Are you national service?'

'Yes, sir, and I was due home for Christmas.'

'Oh, I say, sorry to break it to you like that.'

I was feeling a little better physically, and went for some Tiffin and a large mug of tea. I think the shock had concentrated my mind off my stomach, and I was ready to impart my 'good news' to all the other National Service lads in our gang.

HYCE AND THE TEA MAIDEN

Just over a week after our long day out, on Friday 8 September, we were fit and raring to go on yet another marathon. We duly made our arrangements and chose one of the camp's suggested trips. Approved of by Bobo, we again set sail early after breakfast into the unknown. This trek varied greatly with the others, as we seemed to follow the more level terrain along the mountains, rather than up and down them. Always on this trip we were visually aware of the vast mountain ranges all around us. Although the paths were stony and strewn with boulders, at least we progressed more leisurely and could walk alongside our mules. That is except for one area of solid rock and scree that stretched some distance. Only a shiny, scuff-marked trail showed the best footholds, so we had to sit tight and let the intelligent ones do the walking, occasionally slipping, but they always had another leg to fall back on.

Approaching the village of Hyce, we came to a flat, open plain with cattle and sheep, pine and walnut trees, fields of tall standing maize, and layered dwellings with large flat roofs. We were soon settled in another of Bobo's hideaways, sat out under a canopy of living trees intertwined, and so forming a leafy bower. We sat and rested, smoked and talked, whilst watching a young girl busily prepare our tea in the cooling shade of a huge walnut tree. The fire over which our water boiled sent the smoke gently down the valley. We all sat and watched her sitting within a square of logs, wondering if she was related to Bobo or any other of his comrades. We were served our glasses of tea and purchased for our journey melon, grapes and massive beef tomatoes that were a meal in themselves, as well as boiled eggs and salt. I think that we had brought the bread with us, or some light food pack from the mess, but the addition of fresh food would improve our picnic.

DARACHI GORGE AND CRABS

The next part of our journey took us up to the high ground on top of the mountains, rather than along their sides. This was very rocky, but the muleteers just ran and skipped alongside like mountain goats. Even an older one who must have been at least 45-years-old jumped from rock to boulder. Finally, we ran out of mountain and a huge chasm lay at our feet. The trail led down to the floor of the gorge, and we were soon on our way down to the rushing waters of a wide mountain stream. This was music to our ears. The mules safely tethered in the abundant shade, with running water to drink, we immediately decided to have a dip in the stream before eating. Most stripped off and tested the water, which was cold and woke up the senses. There was little room to swim, even in the largest pool; three strokes and turn, like water trying to find the plughole. After washing the dust and sweat of our journey away, we semi-dried, intent on another dip later, when someone discovered that the pool was infested with tiny crabs. These creatures clung in a rock to rock coating, and so brought our still water-dangling feet quickly to poolside. All were agreed that it was, despite the crabs, a lovely spot; we had enjoyed our dip and most braved the crabs for another swim before we left. The climb back up to the top of the gorge was stony and steep; this brought us to a viewing point from where, on looking down, we could see clearly our lovely crab pools. The towering walls of the gorge were so vertical they looked as if a knife had cut through a slice of cake. We posed for pictures, teetering at the top, and I still recall my relief, once taken, that I could step away from the edge after my staged, nonchalant pose. We retraced our steps and in late afternoon came back to Hyce. On hearing laughing and girlish screams, we sighted at a distance what appeared to be young ladies and girls in the river outside the village. The company thought closer inspection was called for, and a stealthy approach might reward the female-starved Shaibah lads with a little voyeuristic shufti. But the peace was shattered when one of our party let out the battle cry of the republic, and charged Custer-like towards the spot. On arrival, all we saw were ripples in a stream, but it had still been a memorable and beautiful day.

FAREWELL TO LEAVE CAMP

Like all good things, we had to leave, after what had been well over two weeks away from Shaibah and all its luxuries. We were loath to say farewell to a sense of the nomadic lifestyle that we almost touched. Sleeping under the stars, high in the mountains, with riding limbs tired and aching, after some drink, tripping past the tent ropes and the mule corral, dropping into our bunks exhausted. We slept well into the next day to be awakened by the fierce, late-morning sun. We said goodbye to Bobo and the muleteers back down at Babaidi, awaiting their next shipment of raw mule cowboys to break in. The big, brown eyes of Bobo followed our convoy as it left the mule staging post. Strangely, I remember nothing on our return journey of note, except a conversation at the dining car table with a well-dressed, educated, Arab businessman. We mostly talked about our visit to Amadia and our varied trips around there and, of course, the meal before us. He remarked that he did not mind the British as they did not force their religion upon them, and that they would leave eventually anyway. However, I remember very clearly his criticism of our being lazy over languages, to which I had to agree, as our Kurdish store man understood several languages and dialects, but I was still trying to master my own.

We finally arrived back at Shaibah.

Heading for Hyce

Setting out from camp

Heading for Hyce

Hyce

Entering Hyce

Hyce and the tea maiden

Departing Hyce

Roy and Don in the mule corral

Mule train for Darachi Gorge

Arriving Darachi Gorge

Going down the Gorge

Swimming pools and tiny crabs

Darachi Gorge

Don ventures down

Don gets his feet wet

Back up the gorge

Roy, Don, George, Reg and Norman

Darachi – Hyce

Roy, George and I – Darachi Gorge

Hyce with poplars and a field of maize

Hyce

Leaving Hyce

George 'Custer'

Setting out from Camp

Setting out from camp

CHAPTER 16

Shaibah

HOT NIGHTS AND SLEEPING OUT

On approaching Shaibah, I reflected that I was lucky to have had my leave during Shaibah's hottest days, as it had now cooled down to the low hundreds. Sleeping was sometimes difficult with the ceiling fans constantly phut-phutting away, as one tried to keep quite still and calm in an effort to remain cool. Despite the temptation, as many did, to sleep starkers, I always tolerated one sheet and one thin blanket if possible, as the combination of fans and early morning cooling could play havoc and chill your stomach. One answer was to sleep outside the billet, and this many of us preferred to do on hot sultry nights. The bed head was placed next to the billet veranda support, on which the mosquito net was anchored. Then, with all your clothes and footwear stowed inside the net, and well tucked in to foil the tiny invaders, nothing was left on the floor to provide spiders, ants or scorpions with their own bed for the night. There was no light to read by, but we chattered for a while before sleep and were awakened by the bright morning sun as it rounded the corner of the billet. I had a salutary lesson one evening, having gone to the cinema and foolishly left a light on over my bed. On returning, tired and just wanting to drop on my pit, I was horrified to see that the fly door was ajar and my bed alone had attracted millions of small flying creatures. Of course, it was a frantic time, rushing out with bedding, shaking it as far from the billet as possible. Spray cans we did not have, and I had little help from my friends as they were all too busy laughing their heads off. There was always a lot of horseplay and schoolboy humour. One very common trick was to wait until one of your mates had just nodded off to sleep, usually after a drinks night, and ask him

142

quietly in his ear, 'Do you want to buy a battle ship?' On finally getting the message, he would try to ignore it and go back to sleep, but the body does not work like that, and the message hits the bladder. The victim, with the usual expletives, disappears into the night to water the desert. The toilet block was a short distance from the billet and late at night, when an odd piard may be on the prowl, it was the shrubbery in an irrigated bed that had the watery benefits.

SAND YACHTS, SALAMANDER, PELICANS

The Aircraft Fitters and MT Mechanics had between them a few home-made sand yachts, presumably made by the diligent use of the scrapyard, and retiring early the small wheels of aircraft or trailers with some tread still left on the tyres. The Airfield was used by the duty Dakota, the CO's Avro Anson and the occasional visitor, but was empty a lot of the time. We would watch the racing and testing of these craft, but not participate as it was a closed shop. Anyway, I preferred the horses, always have.

One airman caught what, at the time, we were told was a Salamander, and he kept it on a rope lead. Not huge, but with a vicious tail, it was not the best of pets. We never knew what befell this creature as his owner was not the most easy or forthcoming of men. He was reputedly a little punch drunk, or trying to work his ticket and would honk like a seal whilst swimming. Early one morning, whilst I was on guard duty, we were approached by two Baluchi guards returning from a night's vigil. They were going back to their own billets and had attracted a following of curious workers, for these men had bagged a pair of pelicans. They had thought the movements in the bushes were men attempting to get into the camp. After challenging them to come out, they had fired a single warning shot into the bush and hit both birds with the same bullet, or so they claimed. This was followed by most of the Baluchis being laid low with food poisoning following a feast of pelican vindaloo.

AOC'S INSPECTION

If Shaibah had been a ship, you would not say that it was the smartest ship afloat. Not the officers, I hasten to add, but the men did tend to wear their socks around their ankles and were rarely properly dressed. More like the crew of a rust bucket. However, the CO gave us a pep talk, prior to the visit of the AOC, pleading with us to make an effort for the day. The parade assembled at the side of one of the large hangars, thoughtfully in the shade. But by the time the AOC's aircraft had arrived, the sun had sneaked round and was doing its worst to deplete the assembled airmen, and a few wobbled off. However, with a sergeant giving us toe stretching and walking on the spot routines, we just about made it.

We need not have worried, for the AOC had no real criticisms of the lads, but laid into the officers on petty little things. Our section was not excluded from comment, as ministry leaflets about life in the Air Force and advantages of staying on after National Service, with promotion prospects, etc., had been prominently displayed on a notice board.

'What's this all about? After two years they will have made up their minds, they won't need damned leaflets,' the AOC directed at our Equipment Officer. The day following his visit, Flight Lieutenant Wareham, who was a powerfully-built man with some boxing prowess, punched a hole in one of the basket-weave panels of the inner door that led into the main equipment offices. He then punched the back of my pigeon-holed desk, scattering a few unmatched forms to the floor. With a huge smile and a cheery, 'Good morning,' followed by, 'I needed that,' he dispatched the offending leaflets to the bin.

BE SURE YOUR SINS
The road from Shaibah to Basra is not a motorway and in 1950 consisted of a causeway, or steeply banked road, through the low, salt marshland of southern Iraq. I always enjoyed my many trips along this road, just about wide enough for two vehicles to pass, but very little leeway. The travelling Arab, sometimes with livestock, would also add some hazard to the journey. Early morning drives along this road would, without fail, give us strange mirages of palm trees stacked a few layers deep on our left side. We were unable to make out which were the true ones, and which only reflections. After the end of any heavy rain, the marshlands would flood and this gave a sensation of driving on the sea, improving the mirages. Eventually, when the water subsided, the salt gatherers would drive on to the off-white sand and harvest this most precious

desert crop. Many dwellings near Shaibah, and also Basra, had been constructed by an ingenious use of empty jerry cans filled with sand and used as large building blocks in the wall construction. After the flooding, the occupiers could be seen on their roofs, carrying on with their daily chores. They had the same problem annually, but fortunately the floods were not very deep, or severe enough to be life threatening, and the children had something new to play with. Now this road could be an embarrassment, as some of the lads had found to their cost. It was following an unauthorised trip to Basra after a few drinks in the NAAFI, they had borrowed one of the camp's few ambulance vehicles and set off for a night of pleasure. However, on returning late, they had managed to ditch the truck on one of the steeply banked sections of the road and could not budge it. They had a long walk back to camp and had to report their misdemeanour as the truck could be spirited away in the night, and then there would be even more deep poos. The Duty Officer had to awaken the MT section for the towing vehicle to recover it.

CHAPTER 17

Shaibah

'SHAIBAH FOLLIES OF 1950'

Arrangements had been made to provide a show to be held on Thursday 7 December. The highlight for the lads was that five young ladies from RAF Habbaniya were to entertain us. Preparations, stage sets and costumes kept all the non-performing lads busy, whilst the performers rehearsed. One Joe Dade played accordion and I think a banjo, but I remember a group of us sitting in chairs outside the billet as he rehearsed. Then a pedlar selling Amara work of engraved gold and silverware spent the best part of an afternoon trying to sell us all something. Eventually, a few of us did submit; I purchased a silver ring with a gold facing and had my initials engraved thereon. We had bartered for ages and I thought that, at a quarter of the asking price, I had done very well. However, weeks later, the gold started to wear away and the ring easily became oval shaped, and eventually flattened when trodden on. I had to admit that he got the best of the bargain.

Eventually the day came and the show received approval from all, especially for the ladies who were wolf-whistled throughout by bleary-eyed Romeos who fought for a place in the wings. Backstage, as stage door Johnnies, they were eager to engage their eye, and hopefully something more. However, the ladies all disappeared to the officers' quarters, where presumably safer accommodation had been provided for them, and we saw them no more.

CHRISTMAS 1950

My first Christmas at Shaibah I was a newcomer, but now I was amongst established friends, particularly Charlie. He had been married shortly before embarkation and was a regular, counting his days until a home posting would re-unite them later in 1951 at the end of his tour. We started to prepare for the festive season, and an unused small room had been given us by the Equipment Officer to use as the store wallah's exclusive bar. There was great enthusiasm shown in selecting a name for our private bar, but we eventually settled – as we were collectively all store bashers – on calling it 'The Bashers' Rest' and a shield was produced to proclaim it so. The stocking of the bar came from weekly subs, plus a little help from the War surplus perks. Each section had its own bar, of sorts, and everyone circulated around the camp, being welcomed into each one, getting more garrulous and matey with each stop. After Christmas dinner, greetings and requests from home played over the tannoy system. My folks' first choice was not available, so their second choice of the 'Road to the Isles' brought me many Scottish compliments, and the vocal imitations of bagpipes from my fellow Sassenachs.

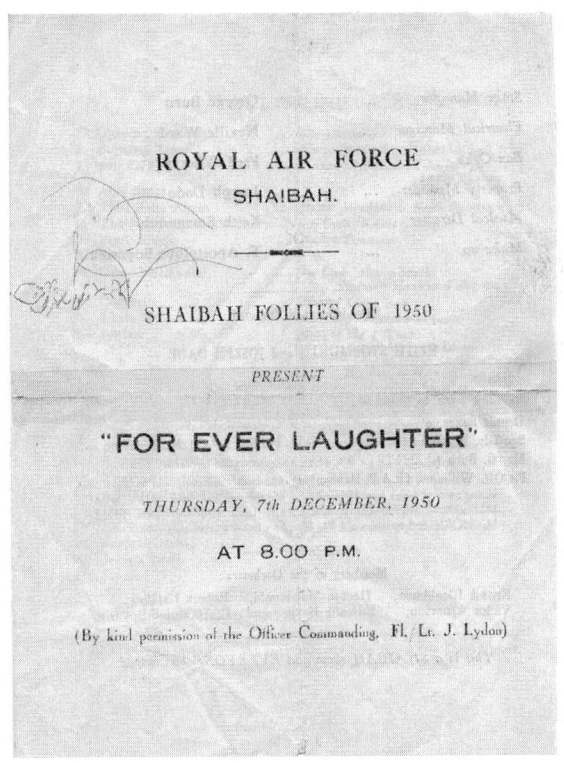

ROYAL AIR FORCE
SHAIBAH.

SHAIBAH FOLLIES OF 1950

PRESENT

"FOR EVER LAUGHTER"

THURSDAY, 7th DECEMBER, 1950

AT 8.00 P.M.

(By kind permission of the Officer Commanding, Fl. Lt. J. Lydon)

Stage Manager	...	...	George Burn
Electrical Manager	...	...	Neville Ward
Box Office	...	...	Fred Wherry
Property Manager	...	...	Joseph Dade
Musical Director	...	...	Keith Stormonth
Make up	...	...	T. Apostolova-Boyarina

Produced and Directed
by
KEITH STORMONTH and JOSEPH DADE

We wish to thank :-

Dennis Baker, a producer until his departure, to whom much is due.
Sqn/Ldr. Mckenna (Garrison Engr.) **Fl/Lt. Phillips** (S.T.O.) **Mr. F. Dyson** and
Mr. G. Burn (of AMWD) for their advice, co-operation and assistance.
Flt/Off. Williams, (R.A.F. Habbaniya) who kindly authorised and arranged the
visiting party of ladies from Habbaniya. We welcome and thank MARY WARD,
MARGARET MAY, ELSIE GASKELL, JUNE HANNA, ANN FALLEN,
Mr. HORN and members of I.A.L. Magil for technical assistance.

Members of the Orchestra :
Ernest Blackburn, Hector Macdonald, Robert Laidlow,
Victor Atherton, Edward Bevin and P. Apostoloff-Boyarin.

This is a SHAIBAH show and EVERYONE has helped.

OVERTURE

1. Opening Chorus	...	*The Company*
2. Dancing Time	...	*Margaret Mays and Bunty Stacey*
3. Balalaika	—	*P. Apostoloff-Boyarin, Joe Dade, Leslie Thomas.*
4. Alan Stead		
5. That Song Again	...	*Hector Macdonald, Keith Stormonth*
6. The Man from the Ministry	...	*Joe Dade, Robert Chapman*
7. Black Magic.	...	*Patrick Donovan*
8. Elsie Gaskell		
9. Cafe Continental	...	*Joe Dade, Harry Smith, Norman Hawkyard and Co.*
10. Concerto	...	*Edward Bevin*
11. Thats News!	...	*Alan Stead, Patrick Donovan*
12. Fanfare	...	*Band of No. 2 Wing, Royal Air Force Levies (by kind permission of Officer Commanding, Wg/Cdr. L. Hamer)*

INTERVAL   15 Minuts

13. King John	...	*Joe Dade, Norman Hawkyard, Ken Tordoff, Bob Thomas and Co.*
14. P. Apostoloff-Boyarin		
15. That Little Something	...	*Joe Dade, Ken Tordoff*
16. A Night at the Angel	...	*The Company*
17. Dear old Shaibah	...	*Keith Stormonth, Bill Phillips*
18. Conversation Pieces	...	*George Davison, Bob Thomas*
19. Surprise Item		
20. Joseph Dade		
21. Finale	...	*The Company*

GOD SAVE THE KING

This Company includes :- Bob Galbraith, Bob Ison, Bob White, Brian Glover,
George Dyson, Bob Gibbons, Bob Hird.

Sergeant's football team

Charlie pipped in 220yds

'The Bashers' Rest'

Band of No.2 Wing – Royal Air Force levies

ROYAL AIR FORCE STATION

SHAIBAH

IRAQ COMMAND

———

Programme and Menu

CHRISTMAS DAY. 1950

———

The Commanding Officer
Flight Lieutenant C. Lydon
and Officers wish all ranks
A Very Happy Christmas.

Christmas Day Menu.

08-00 — 9-00 Hours
BREAKFAST
Cornflakes with Milk
Grilled Bacon — Fried Eggs on Toast
Baked Beans and Tomatoe Sauce
Tea and Coffee

13.00 Hours
CHRISTMAS DINNER
Creme of Tomatoe Soup
Roast Turkey - Roast Goose
Roast Duck - Roast Pork
Sauce Demmi Glase' - Bread Sauce
Apple Sauce
Stuffing
Roast Potatoes - Boiled Potatoes
Cauliflower and Green Peas
Christmas Pudding and Brandy Sauce
Mince Pies
Nuts - Apples - Oranges - Bananas
Cigarettes and Beer

17.00 Hours
BUFFET TEA
Assorted Game Sandwiches - Assorted Rolls
Pine Apple Fritters - Chocolate Eclairs
Cream Doughnuts - Fancy Sponges
Evelyn Buns - Jellies - Cream Chantilly
Tea

CHRISTMAS ATTRACTIONS

Christmas Day

10.00 HOURS

Fancy Dress Football Match
Officers Mess versus Sergeants Mess

11.00 HOURS

Billet Bars
*Inspection and judging by Commanding Officer
and presentation of prizes*

14.15 HOURS

Letters from Home
*A Programme of Greetings and request records
from your loved ones at home*

EVENING

GO AS YOU PLEASE

Boxing Day

10.30 HOURS

ALL THE FUN OF THE FAIR – STATION GYMNASIUM
Booths — Sideshows — To Test your Skill

SPECIAL ATTRACTION
The Linforth Boxing Booth — Featuring the
following Knock-out attractions

CARNERA DAVIDSON   v   MAN MOUNTAIN SMITH
HORIZONTAL HIND   v   BRUISER BROWN
and that Clash of Giants
A.L. PHILLIPS   v   LARRY LARKIN
(The Shaibah Tiger)   *(The Battling Grocer)*

14.15 HOURS

SHAIBAH RACES
to be held
ON THE STATION SPORTS GROUND
Licenced Bookmakers. (Chained Down) and
Full Tote Facilities
*The racing Mules have been specially trained for this event
which will be run
under National Greyhound Racing Association Rules*
Bumping — Boring and Binding Barred

19.30 HOURS
CINEMA SHOW

Enjoying a melon

Jim and I

Charlie and Geordie

Mac and I

Outer Camp – empty billets

Charlie takes a cuppa

Syd Sawyer *Louis Brown and Ken Way*

Jim, Louis, Ken, Geordie, Dick and Juma

Syd, Charlie and Les

A thirst quencher

Charlie and Mac

Shadow handshake

Self and Jim

Charlie, Mac and I

In the morning after our 'special' breakfast of cornflakes, bacon, egg and beans, we were invited to attend a fancy dress football match; officers v. sergeants. This was preceded by the band of No. 2 wing, Royal Air Force levies, giving a stirring musical curtain-raiser to the match. After the match, some of the other ranks challenged the officers and sergeants to a hockey match. Now our bullish Equipment Officer had remarked to Charlie, 'I thought hockey was a girls' game,' and Charlie, during the game, committed an 'accidental' foul with his stick on the said officer, causing him much pain. Charlie walked off the field with an exaggerated wide grin on his face. Later on, we had comic boxing with oversized gloves and nothing was taken seriously. Then Christmas dinner was served by the officers, including turkey, goose, duck and pork, of which we stuffed ourselves silly. This at least should provide a bed to absorb some of the afternoon's drinking. We also had mule races in the afternoon, but I can't, for some reason, recall them. The day finished with a cinema show at 7.30pm, followed by further bar visiting until our legs gave out.

IT STICKS TO BLANKETS

The Christmas period was spread over several days of eating and drinking, but still had to accommodate some vital duties, and the roster included guard duties and, of course, air control. The lads of air control could not get one of their section to sober up long enough to let him take on his responsible and life-dependent role. As a result, the other lads were not having much fun covering all of his shifts. It required serious deliberation, and it was decided to catch the lad and sober him up, but how? Then someone had the brainwave of confining him to bed for a few hours, before forcibly administering black coffee. So his bed was placed centre-room and he was then held down carefully cocooned in his own blanket, so that only his head and pinkies were visible. With borrowed belts, we then tied him up like a spring roll and departed to the NAAFI. After a few hours, we returned to wash and collect our mugs and eating irons for Tiffin. As we entered the billet, an almighty over-powering pong brought us back to our unfinished business, as the lad, being unable to trip to the loo, had managed without. The immediate thought was to do a runner, but no one was allowed to and we were all needed to carry him and his blanket out to the wash house, and slowly peel our ripe parcel. Here we let the shower and a broom or two brush away as best we could, until at least he was clean enough for dry clothes. The blanket took us and our billet boys a few days to clean, for we had found out the hard way that it really does stick to blankets.

Bang on New Year's Day, I achieved the heady rank of LAC.

CHAPTER 18

Bahrain

THE PERSIAN GULF

It was sometime in April 1951 that I had my second leave and the opportunity to visit the Royal Air Force Base at Muharraq, a small island joined to the northernmost tip of Bahrain by a causeway to its capital Manama. This leave had coincided with some courses or exams, requiring a movement of airmen between camps, for as well as the Duty Dakota, the station Avro Anson was to be used, and we did not fancy a flight in the Anson. The aircraft fitters always grumbled that the CO brought it back needing lots of remedial work, which did not inspire confidence. Tony and I managed to get aboard the Dakota thanks to Roy, who I think was in charge of the aircraft payloads, by making sure we were not on the Anson. The balancing of payloads had been roughly explained to me. I had actually helped in strapping and battening down equipment shipped by the Dakota on some previous occasions. We settled down to a flight that took us over the remaining miles of southern Iraq, over the Shatt al Arab to its entry into the Persian Gulf. At this stage, the aircraft caught the thermals, which felt like a sudden descent by a pit shaft cage, and I know what they mean by heart in your mouth. Apparently, this happened most of the year over this land to water area, and we wondered how the Anson would have differed. The blue waters of the Persian Gulf below, with the bright contrasting glare of sand of the Kuwaiti and then Saudi desert beaches, made exciting viewing. The approach to Muharraq I can recall vividly as we circled to land on this small island spread-out below. Completely encircled by shallow translucent water of a pale turquoise, and shimmering in the sun, it was Ballantynes' *The Coral Island,* there for me to explore.

RAF MUHARRAQ

The accommodation at the camp was, as I recall, in small separate rooms and not in a communal billet. This was a pleasant change, and the first privacy I had experienced since joining the RAF. And it was not under canvas as at Ser-Amadia; the room also had a framed picture of a cottage garden, to make one feel at home. The camp's facilities were not a great deal more than at Shaibah, but the sight of the blue gulf waters made a welcome change from the dry desert. At least civilisation, in the form of Manama, capital of Bahrain, was only a few miles down the causeway. Years later, the island of Bahrain was also joined to the Saudi Arabian mainland by a long causeway. The camp had a smaller swimming pool than Shaibah, and a game of water polo that I joined in had to have special rules as the goalkeeper's throw could reach the other net with ease, especially the one in the shallow end. The ocean always looked so inviting for a swim, but we were advised that a certain small fish caused you problems inshore, and sharks could end your problems further out. So we were content to explore the island and found that on the far side of the airstrip was a Sultan's summer palace, but we were not invited.

RAF Muharraq

RAF station at Muharraq

Me and my Brownie box camera

Tony snaps me

Muharraq

RAF lads with their homemade sailboat

Causeway Road to Manama

Bahrain

Bahrain – Sons of Sinbad

Manama – Bahrain

In search of footprints in the sand

Inspecting a Muharraq well

Feluccas and fishing nets

Portuguese Fort

Palms at rear of Fort

The Persian Gulf – sunset memories

Bahrain – Sons of Sinbad

The airfield was much busier than at Shaibah, for this was a strategic link in the flying routes even then, and it had a constant buzz about it. On the camp there was a desalination plant, and the first thing we had to adjust to was the extreme humidity of the place, and the salty tastes. At lunch time we ate our meal in the mess hall, but carried back to our rooms the steaming mug of hot, salty, bromide tea. Then, stripped off to drink our beverage, we literally watched the sweat emerge from every pore. Towelling down to a bearable dampness, we rested until cool enough to dress. The cold drinks in the NAAFI also tasted of salt; it seemed superfluous to have been issued with salt tablets. There were some small sailing dinghies, mainly self-made by the resident airmen. Much as Shaibah had its sand yachts, the resourceful servicemen had made the most of their situation. The camp itself reached out to the gulf waters, and a long concrete pathway stretched out on top of a sewage pipe. To stroll along this gave some good views of the camp, and the little island. My favourite memory here was sitting at sundown by the water's edge with its cooling breezes, enjoying the very beautiful sunsets across the Gulf.

ALADDIN'S CAVE IN MANAMA

It was possible to walk from the RAF base to Bahrain's capital and port city of Manama, by a long straight causeway. This gave us the opportunity to see across the Persian Gulf and the busy sea lanes of ocean-going ships. Much nearer were the dhows and feluccas, both at sea and also at anchor. Some were tied to the wharfs with barefoot crews, preparing to set sail for Basra, Abadan, Kuwait, or down to Sharjah, or further still to Muscat. Some could be engaged on pearl fishing, but they all evoked the images of Sinbad and his colourful adventures. Now Manama brought us nearer to home, as there were car showrooms and large shops, but we headed for the souk or bazaar in the more down-market areas, which were more in keeping with our pockets. After wandering around for some considerable time, seeing many desirable items outside our reach, a little wearied, we were invited into one of the larger shops by an Indian merchant. This gentleman was gently persuasive and he brushed aside our protests that we had no money for his very beautiful goods, and were but admiring them from afar. He graciously thanked us for our complimentary remarks, and asked us to come inside and see the rest of his stock. We entered and were astonished at the wealth of all manner of carpets, jewel boxes and jewelled daggers. And spread before us, alas, a huge tiger skin, its eyes fixed with a sadness that would not get better. The talking and tea drinking went on for some time. Tony and I and two others from the camp were all fascinated by both the man and his shop. There were carved ivory caskets and sandalwood boxes, mostly of Indian origin. After a while, we all found something to buy and, as I would soon be homeward bound, I chose two wall carpets that stood out as bright and cheerful. One was of lions, to remind me of the entrance to Basra and the other of camels, for obvious reasons. For myself, I purchased a small, handmade knife with its curved blade, sliding into a sandalwood leather-covered sheath; of this I was quite pleased. On close inspection of the carpets back at camp, I discovered that 'Made in Italy' was stamped on its Hessian back; not a very oriental capture. One other item purchased from another shop was a pram cover, for I was soon to become an uncle. What colour should I choose? There was only blue or pink, so I chose blue, and luckily it was a boy. It would have been a long trip to make an exchange, had he been a she.

FOOTPRINTS AND PORTUGUESE FORTS

Now greedy wants more and, with help again from our payload chums, we had connived to extend our leave by at least a few days, by putting ourselves on low priority for the return flight. Airmen being posted or on essential training, plus vital equipment all took precedence; alas, there was no room for us on the originally booked flight, so we settled back and continued to enjoy our extended leave. I believe it was a Sunday morning, for I had not dated my Bahrain snaps. But it felt like a Sunday morning walk, with Tony and another lad whom we palled up with, no name recalled, but very good company. Our walk from camp to the other side of a small bay or lagoon took all of that morning. On the way along this sandy shoreline, we fooled about looking for Man Friday's footprints, and doing a sort of cannibal war dance, for there was no one around; it was peacefully people-free. On the far side, we came to the square-shaped huts of the local fishermen whose nets were stretched out to trap the ebb-tide fish heading for the dinner plate. Drying nets hung from high poles down to the water in graceful drapes, like a scene from *Sanders of the River*. I could picture Paul Robeson singing his famous canoe song as he paddled past. The Portuguese occupied Bahrain up to 1602, and therefore the fort ruins that we came upon, built by them, were in remarkable shape. To the rear of the forts were palm trees in abundance, and we spent a few childish moments picking off the advancing hordes of Tuaregs. All this before making our way back along the beach for dinner, and perhaps a cooling afternoon siesta. This was the life.

THE BEST LAID PLANS

Approaching the camp, we were quickly informed that the tannoys had been blaring out our names for hours; apparently my beloved Equipment Officer had not taken kindly to our extended leave. He had searched the air lanes for some transport to return me to my little desk as quickly as possible. Unfortunately, he commissioned an aircraft from Karachi testing air control approaches of the airfields, to drop in at Muharraq and pick us up. We therefore just about had time to grab a little food, shower, pack our bags and rush up to the runway to await the arrival of our airborne taxi. The aircraft approached and taxied right up to us, upon which the door opened and out stepped the pilot and some crew. The engines had not been switched off, someone's cheese-cutter hat had done a flyer and we had to make a quick dash to recover same. The pilot said, 'Where are these bloody VIPs, I told them I could not wait about.' Tony said, 'I think we are the only passengers, sir.' He seemed relieved that his passengers were not important and so fighting the propellers' dusty wind, we climbed aboard and said goodbye to our island in the sun.

The aircrew made us most welcome. Not for the first time, I was to fly with only a select few on a large aircraft over splendid landscapes. To charter such a flight would cost a fortune today if these throbbing monsters were still around. The crew, mainly checking out results of tests made so far, explained that the skipper was a little concerned about one of his engines. Hence his reluctance to switch off the engines on picking us up and if we saw smoke, or anything amiss, to let them know. How much was bull for our benefit, their private joke, or was it a realistic concern? They said that the skipper was weighing up whether it would be better to ditch in the sea close to land and try to out-swim the sharks, or try to find a flat strip of desert and not smash up the kite. I think they overplayed it a little. We reached Shaibah after an enjoyable trip, alighted with engines still running, holding on to our hats and waved our transport goodbye.

CHAPTER 19

Shaibah

GUARDING THE PIGGERY

During the period of my tour there were troubled theatres of hostilities, and warfare in Vietnam and Korea. But these were far enough away not to affect us, except perhaps the extension of six months more service to do. However, the Iranians were about to nationalise the oil interests at Abadan, and this was not too far away. The bullish owners were taking part in fighting talk, and it became a possibility that we could come in and play a part. There was talk of evacuating the oil workers and their families to dear old Shaibah. The unused, half-submerged huts in the outer camp area would be ideal, after evicting the creepy-crawlies, scorpions and snakes that may have taken up residence there. We airmen, however, had now to be honed into a sort of defensive force, to guard and protect our camp from attack. So when an alarm was sounded, we were all to muster outside the armoury and collect our weapons. This we did in orderly fashion, collecting our Lea Enfield 303s, plus a couple of clips of ammunition, signed a book, and regrouped outside to await further instructions. Whisky, our dog, could not understand this late night activity and barked his head off, especially at any civilian Arabs or uniformed levies around. We were then allocated our pre-numbered guard posts, and I should have known that I was to be allocated, with others, to the pigsty turret full of bloody memories. None of us relished finding out what the interior looked like and all promised to come back in the daytime and do a bit of spring cleaning. So our guard duty, for now, was conducted outside the blockhouse, looking out over Blondie's and the piggies' last resting place, and the outer camp where we did most of our riding. The all-clear sounded and we returned our firepower to the armoury, and made haste to try and get a little sleep. Now we knew our post and cleaned it up pretty good, and we did not encounter any big nasties. We had about another two call-outs, and quite liked the night time diversion. Then the troubles passed as far as we were concerned, and no more blockhouse guards were necessary.

RISQUÉ SONGS AND JOKES

Balmy evenings outside the NAAFI, especially on pay night, would find tables of airmen singing and joking until the early hours. Mac, in particular, would produce his repertoire of recitations and ballads, such as 'The Bachelors Lament'. One verse explains the sentiment:

> There once was a bachelor,
> Who lived with his son?
> And worked at the weavers trade,
> And the only, only, thing that he ever did wrong,
> Was to woo, a fair young maid.

This could be followed by a recitation of 'Mad Carew' or 'The Green Eye of the Little Yellow God' which has about eleven verses. The aforementioned were not in any way vulgar, but the indignities that befell Old Riley's daughter certainly were.

Jokes came in many variations and the Medical Officer at El Hamra had told a couple during his lecture on avoiding the usual diseases. New recruits to the Camel Corps had just been told that they were ready to train on camels, and that they would be their closest companions in the months ahead, and they would ride, eat and sleep with them in the desert. The camels were brought in and a stampede of recruits raced to get their camels.

'What's the hurry?' asked one.

'You don't want to get an ugly one do you?' was the reply.

Recruits were also told of the dangers of the Middle East fleshpots and stressing, that for half an hour of pleasure, you may reap a lifetime of misery. At this, one excited youth put up a hand.

'Yes, airman?'

'Well, sir! How do you make it last half an hour?'

TICKING OFF THE DAYS

When a serviceman approaches the end of his tour, he becomes demob-happy, and starts to tick off on a calendar each day that passes, which is a right little pain to those with still a lot to do. I really enjoyed my stay at Shaibah. I know the old cliché, remembering only the good times is true. But there was a special bond, due to the isolation, miles from outside distractions; we made the best of what we had. I took a book-keeping course that the Education Officer arranged, and others also took various courses, although on hot days it took some doing. There were many sporting activities; Charlie played hockey and was a good runner, and he came second to the blonde Adonis on one occasion, pipped by a whisker. I could outrun him for very short bursts, but then got out of puff; however, the dry desert heat had, I think, been very beneficial to my health. Apart from my bronchial pneumonia early on, I had enjoyed rude health. Shaibah had some tennis courts, two for the men, and I think the officers had their own. The common ones were protected on one side against the prevailing winds by a sandy brick wall that disin-tegrated during the hurricane of May 1950, and was hastily rebuilt a little stronger. There were still days when the wind affected one side so fiercely that it was like playing uphill. There were, of course, the guard duties and on one occasion, I had to take over from the Duty Clerk who was off on a trip to the consul in Basra. He returned well after midnight, for he must have had the Duty Driver with a girl in Asher. On walking back to my billet in the early hours, a levy on patrol frightened the life out of me by leaping out with rifle cocked, demanding identification. I quickly produced my pay book, and then stood talking with him for a long time, having a smoke, for he was obviously a new recruit and very keen. A more experienced guard would have waited until I was in a lit area, to see if he recognised me. We often shared a smoke and a chat with the patrolling guards on the SHQ verandah, keeping a wary eye out for the Duty Officer. The night could be long and lonely, as Duty Clerk was a one-man vigil, with only a Sten gun for company.

FAREWELLS

The day arrived for my departure, homeward-bound at last! Greatly excited by the thought of family reunions in a few days' time, my kit was packed early and after breakfast I took a walk through the camp to take a last look. Firstly the main gate; no more guard duties or thoughts of riding out to the Zubair oil rigs, and Blondie's nervy ride. On the way back to the left the scrap and surpluses compound, and then the kerosene compound, where scorpions liked to nest among the drums. The powerful fuel scenting the air, that I recall even now; on hot days at petrol stations my thoughts wander back. The armoury, firing range and SHQ were on the right; the MT and equipment sections to the left. A walk to the airstrip and aircraft fitter's workshop, the hangar where pay parades and the sale of contraband cigarettes took place. Then you passed the outdoor and indoor cinema and theatre, the officers' quarters, and finally the stables, where I had probably had my happiest moments, and also the saddest. I took leave of Hamad, Peter and Bill. Finally, there was a swimming tournament taking place on the day of my departure and Charlie was involved. When the time came for me to head for the airstrip, Charlie was in a water polo match and managed to swim to the side and bid me farewell with a wet handshake. There were so many farewells, from billet and section lads and, of course, Mahli and Hamet, but the wet handshake I recall the most.

LYNEHAM

VIA EL ADEM AND IDRIS

I hastened to collect my kit and struggled to the airstrip to wait with the others for my longest air trip to date, some 3,500 miles or more. The start was not impressive as, once aboard, the skipper apologised and asked us all to disembark and wait in the shade of the wings as the fitters had to do some work on the aircraft. We sat, or sprawled, in the cool for some considerable time. I seem to recall that we set off and called at Habbaniya for a short stop, and then flew non-stop to North Africa. I do remember that on our descent at El Adem, I happened to be forward, able to get a pilot's eye view of the landing. It was now night and the runway lights were visible from a long way off. The descent was a magical experience to me. At RAF El Adem, Idris (or Castel Benito), some twenty miles south of Tobruk, it can be very cold at night. We had arrived in our lightweight summer kit, being in the 80s when leaving Shaibah, hot and sweaty. But now we grabbed our kit-bags and pulled out our heavy blues and made for the ablution block for a quick change for we were visibly shivering. There was a meal and NAAFI facilities afterwards, before re-embarking for our final hop. The flight over the Mediterranean at night was followed by a cloudy passage all the way back to England, so we were cheated out of our first sight of the coast of Blighty that we all longed to see. Landing at RAF Lyneham, at an early hour in pouring rain was not the best of ways to come home. We had to come through customs and declare any valuables, cigarettes, etc., but on an LAC's pay, there was little chance to have an excess of the former.

One lad had an excess of watches all up his arms; another the latest in expensive cameras. Both airmen had, I think, come from Karachi or Bahrain. There, such goods were more easily obtained than at Shaibah's souk, and they were marched off for closer inspection. My turn came to declare and said I had nothing.

'No camera?' he asked.

'Only an old one I took out with me,' I replied.

'May I see it?' he asked.

I delved in my pack and produced my faithful companion, a battered old Kodak box brownie, black and white camera for all to inspect. One look and he chalked my bag. I may have been embarrassed then, but now I value its time with me. All the memories that I brought back of my two years' National Service are all the more vivid for its honesty.

HEDNESFORD

GREEN FIELDS OF ENGLAND

We were processed out of Lyneham and arrived at RAF Hednesford in the late afternoon in pouring rain. We collected our bedding and made for our billet. This was cold and damp, not at all what we had been used to. A shivering corporal said 'Let's get some bloody coal,' and a party went foraging with buckets pinched from adjacent empty billets. Soon they had returned, and had found the NAAFI coal supply and a wooden crate. With everyone eagerly wafting papers for draught and with smoke everywhere, coughing and spluttering, we obtained a massive fire with bits of crate sticking out and burning bits falling about the floor. These we just kicked off the floorboards back against the fire, all encircled the glare and tried to dry off. Welcome home! The next priority after the cookhouse and NAAFI was to try and get some sleep. No telephoning home; this was 1951 and not many homes had them. At the earliest next morning, I was up with all other the lads who lived within striking distance. As this was Sunday, and demob leave did not commence until Monday, after certain rituals such as demob suits, etc., getting home for Sunday lunch was the priority. After a hurried breakfast, I started to walk to Rugeley. It was a fair way, so I was very pleased to be offered a lift in an open-top sports car by some officer who had spotted me escaping. I had about an hour or more to wait for the next bus, and realised that the climatic changes I had undergone during the last few days, not least the wet billet, had produced the worst kind of cold and sore throat imaginable. It had taken me about a month to travel out to Shaibah and get acclimatised from cold to very hot. But the return journey, hot to very cold, took a couple of days only. Eventually travelling the last of my journey in dry weather, I could see green fields and trees, so in contrast to the glare of the desert sand. I finally arrived home, and then with the hugs and kisses of loved ones, I was welcomed back into the fold.

'You're not very brown, are you?' said Mother, looking at my weary, cold, drained face. 'No, I suppose I'm not,' I croaked. But the sight of lamb, fresh-shelled garden peas and new potatoes (not reconstituted) and mint sauce, told me I was home.

About the Author

Born on Friday 13th February 1931 and snowing, I was told. I had two brothers and one sister. Brother David came later. Mother was the eldest of 11 children, so I had plenty of aunts and uncles, living mainly in Tamworth, Nuneaton, or Market Bosworth. Although a town dweller, I had plenty of country experience; strawberry, pea and bean picking, with trips to Stratford and Evesham to obtain items not grown themselves that were for sale at the Saturday market at Nuneaton. I also took part in selling at the stall whilst my uncle and aunt had taken a lunch break.

My father's family was smaller, a sister and a brother, as he had lost his elder brother in France, who died of his wounds in August 1916. Then Father went to France and served his time as a machine gunner and being a single man, he had remained behind for some time, looking after the horses, etc, whilst the married men went home. During the World War II, he spent time in the home guard, also fire watching for the post office in Solihull.

The early years were a mixture of growing up in a wartime environment and recurring bouts of pneumonia or pleurisy, both very painful. These left me a little short of breath, but determined to put my physical weakness aside, I spent a lot of time cycling, canoeing and rowing at the many parks, rivers and canals that surrounded Birmingham, when councils provided parks with tennis courts, putting greens and boating facilities, we did not have the easier options of using ones digits on a computer game.

The arrival of my brother David in the period of the Birmingham blitz, required us to evacuate to Nuneaton for a short spell, when a bomb hit the water mains and we were on temporary stand pipes, but we did not avoid the air raids as enemy aircraft attacked Coventry nearby and we sampled aunty's shelter. A bomb was dropped in a nearby field and created a large pond that we stocked with tadpoles and minnows over the ensuing months.

I still recall the day the air raid warden delivered our gas masks, especially the one for our new addition, and helping Mother to place David in the big grey device that had a large plastic screen and side bellows, it was not a pleasant task. Days were spent searching for shrapnel, incendiary tail fins, etc. Our neighbour had an incendiary embedded in the mound of soil at the rear of the Anderson shelter and for a time enjoyed the warmth, until realising the reason for the change in temperature.

Then finally, I had my call up and although it was hard work, I had to prove to myself physically, that I was able to step up to the plate. The change of climate in Iraq was mainly dry and I feel it helped, I remember my time there with good memories of fun and comradeship. After demob, I returned to my job of audit clerk in the city, enjoying the diversity of visiting many factories and shops, learning a little of each trade from button manufacture to heavy iron floor mouldings for tank turrets, a motor cycle factory, glassmaking and jewellery, here in Birmingham, the city of a thousand trades; who said accountancy was boring?

I would like to thank all those who are in my photos, the many friends and comrades who contribute to the telling of my book. Those who triggered off the publication of my work and were kind enough to say they enjoyed the read. Then later to be shown a copy of The Habbite for the first time in 2016, I became aware of the interest still shown in the RAF camps of Habbaniya and other camps including Shaibah. By chance, my neighbour revealed that he had a friend whose work was published by Melrose Books and obtained their telephone number, the rest is history.

Beryl, my wife and companion – on honeymoon at Bournemouth

Sons – Richard and John in the sand dunes at Aberdovey

IN GRANDDAD'S BOOK – JACK, ISABEL AND CARA

Jack and partner, Shelby, have repeatedly asked me to try and publish the book. Jack for a very long time, as I had related my tales at bedtime, together with *Coral Island* or *Treasure Island*, when he and Isabel were little, so thanks to your support, Jack, here it is as promised.

Our family has been going to Aberdovey since the 1930's when Granddad first went there with his Mom and Dad. Thank you, Granddad, for sharing with me your special place. This, too, will become my special place, and will be passed down to future generations. Love you, Isabel.

With love from Cara